Frederick Theodore Frelinghuysen

Some of the Speeches delivered by Fred'k T. Frelinghuysen

Frederick Theodore Frelinghuysen

Some of the Speeches delivered by Fred'k T. Frelinghuysen

ISBN/EAN: 9783337154233

Printed in Europe, USA, Canada, Australia, Japan

Cover: Foto ©ninafisch / pixelio.de

More available books at **www.hansebooks.com**

SOME OF THE SPEECHES

DELIVERED BY

FRED'K T. FRELINGHUYSEN,

OF NEW JERSEY,

IN THE

SENATE OF THE UNITED STATES

DURING THE

First Session of the Forty Fourth Congress.

WASHINGTON, D. C.:
JUDD & DETWEILER, PRINTERS AND PUBLISHERS.
1876.

TABLE OF CONTENTS.

THE SCHOOL AMENDMENT.

The Senate proceeded to consider the joint resolution (II. R. No. 1) proposing an amendment to the Constitution of the United States, the pending question being on its passage—

Mr. FRELINGHUYSEN said :

Mr. President, before the vote is taken on this measure, I propose to state the principles involved in it, and to do so with great brevity.

There are only two principles involved in this article for the amendment of the Constitution, as passed by the House or as now amended by the Senate :

I. That there shall be no establishment of religion or prohibition of the free exercise thereof, and that there shall be no religious test as a qualification to office in the several States of the Union.

II. That the people shall not be taxed to promote the particular creed or tenets of any religious or anti-religious sect or denomination.

Let me remark that it is manifest that the people call for an amendment covering these two principles. This is manifest from the fact that the Representatives of the people of every religious and political persuasion, coming fresh from every section of the country, have by a vote of 166 out of 171 (only 5 negatives) declared that to be the will of the people.

Further, sir ; on the passage by the House of this amendment, which undertook to affirm and to protect these two principles, and which the people and the press, and which I assume the House of Representatives thought was effective, great gratification was afforded to the whole country, not only because of their wish that these principles should be incorporated in our fundamental law, but also because this vexed question was to be removed from the arena of party politics. The great unanimity of the vote in the House shows how strong is the conviction of the Representatives of the people that this article of amendment to the Constitution is within the legitimate province of constitutional amendments, and is also in accord with the best policy and the soundest interests of the nation.

There is, sir, no room for two opinions on the two propositions that religion and conscience should be free, and that the people should not be taxed for sectarian purposes. The whole history of our country, from its origin to the present day, establishes and fortifies these positions. And nothing can be clearer than that these fundamental rights should be secured in a constitution ordained expressly to " establish justice " and to " secure the blessings of liberty."

Mr. President, while the two principles of religious freedom and exemption from taxation for sectarian purposes are plainly asserted in the article as it comes to us from the House, there are, unfortunately, in it defects and omissions that were it accepted, without amendment, by the States would render it nugatory and invalid. And the House should be gratified that a more careful scrutiny has discovered and corrected these defects, and should be ready to concur at once in the amendment of the Senate. I will point out these defects and their corrections.

I. The fifth article of the Constitution requires that Congress when proposing amendments to the Constitution shall state to the people in what manner the amendment shall be ratified ; whether by the Legislatures of the States or by conventions in the States ; the fifth article is as follows :

" The Congress, whenever two-thirds of both Houses shall deem it necessary, shall pro-
" pose amendments to this Constitution, or on the application of the Legislatures of two-
" thirds of the several States, shall call a convention for proposing amendments, which,
" In either case, shall be valid to all intents and purposes, as part of this Constitution,
" when ratified by the Legislatures of three-fourths of the several States, or by conven-
" tions in three-fourths thereof, as the one or the other mode of ratification may be pro-
" posed by the Congress."

This article amending the Constitution as it came from the House failed to propose either mode of ratifying this amendment. It did not propose that it should be ratified by the Legislatures or that it should be ratified by conventions. Had the Legislatures ratified it, not being in conformity with the requirements of the Constitution, it would have been invalid.

I call the attention of the Senate to the first alteration the House amendment makes in our Constitution. The first amendment to the Constitution, enacted shortly after the adoption of the Constitution, provides that—

"Congress shall make no law respecting an establishment of religion, or prohibiting "the free exercise thereof."

This is an inhibition on Congress, and not on the States. The House article very properly extends the prohibition of the first amendment of the Constitution to the States. But the sixth article of the old Constitution also provides that—

"No religious test shall ever be required as a qualification to any office or public trust "under the United States."

This provision, in such close harmony with the first amendment of the Constitution, the House article entirely omits, and it has very properly been inserted by the Senate and made applicable to the States.

Nobody can object to the Senate amendment on account of these two positions contained in it.

Thus the article as amended by the Senate prohibits the States, for the first time, from the establishment of religion, from prohibiting its free exercise, and from making any religious test a qualification to office.

II. Now, as to the second division of the proposed article amending the Constitution relative to the use of the public money for sectarian purposes, let me say that there are six different modes by which the people can be taxed for sectarian purposes.

1. By appropriating money raised for school purposes to sectarian schools.
2. By appropriating money from the general treasury to sectarian schools.
3. By appropriating public money to sectarian institutions other than schools, as theological institutions, sectarian colleges, monasteries, and nunneries.
4. By devoting schools or other institutions established by public funds, when so established, to sectarian purposes.
5. By making appropriations of public money to religious denominations, or to promote their interests.
6. By appropriating public money to an institution to promote infidelity or for the benefit of an anti-religious sect.

The amendment of the Senate guards against all these abuses, while the article as it came from the House only prohibited the first, to wit, the appropriation of public money, and only public money raised for schools, to sectarian schools or dividing it among denominations.

The Senate amendment only carries out the principle and cures the defects of the article as it came from the House, but it does so effectually.

Why, sir, provide that money raised for schools shall not be appropriated to sectarian schools, and leave it lawful to appropriate to sectarian schools from the general treasury?

Why should we prohibit appropriations to sectarian schools, and yet permit schools established by the public money to be made sectarian?

Why prohibit appropriations to sectarian schools and permit money to be appropriated to sectarian institutions of another character? Why prohibit appropriations to religious sects and permit them to be made to infidel sects?

There is no reason; and any one who could honestly and sincerely vote for the article as it came from the House, should rejoice in the opportunity of voting for the Senate amendment.

Not only does the article as it came from the House merely apply to the appropriation of money raised for schools to sectarian purposes, but it omits to give Congress any power by legislation to prevent or punish the violations of the article.

The usual section conferring power on Congress by legislation to enforce an amendment, is in these words :

"Congress shall have power to enforce this article by appropriate legislation."

But as the committee were aware that some might argue that such a section would confer on Congress the power to interfere with public schools of the States, the committee, to avoid all possible objection, have—though they were satisfied that an article so phrased would not have the effect claimed—reported a section which gives no affirmative power to Congress, but simply provides that—

"Congress shall have power, by appropriate legislation, to provide for the prevention and punishment of violations of this article."

This section takes the place of the strange provision of the article as it came from the House, which is in these words :

"This article shall not vest, enlarge, or diminish legislative power in Congress."

Some have called this House article the Blaine amendment. No such provision was ever suggested by that distinguished man. He left the article to be enforced under the provisions of the original Constitution, which (article 1, section 8, placit 18) provides—

"That Congress shall have power 'to make all laws which shall be necessary and proper "for carrying into execution the foregoing powers and all other powers vested by this "Constitution in the Government of the United States, or in any department or officer "thereof;' and this article is to be part of this Constitution."

This article when adopted, by the very terms of the fifth article of the Constitution, becomes, in the language of the Constitution, "to all intents and purposes a part of the Constitution." Now the provision as it comes from the House prevents the provision of the old Constitution, which I have read, from operating, for it declares that "nothing in this article shall be held to vest, enlarge, or diminish any legislative power in Congress." So that Congress would have no more power over the subject after the passage of the article than it had before it was passed, while the section introduced in the Senate amendment limits the power of the old Constitution by making a specific provision that Congress shall have power over this subject so far as to prevent and punish violations of this article.

Mr. President, it has been said that this amendment will prevent religious instruction in our prisons and other institutions supported by the public revenue. The clause which is relied upon to maintain that position is this :

"And no such particular creed or tenets "—

That is, no particular creed or tenets—

"of any religious or anti-religious sect or denomination shall be read or taught in any "school or institution supported in whole or in part by such "—

That is public—

"revenue."

Sir, does that prohibit religious instruction in prisons ? Does it prevent religious instruction anywhere? If the visit to those who are sick and in prison is for the purpose of reading to them or of teaching them the particular creed or tenets of a religious or anti-religious sect or denomination, this article does interfere with it, and is designed to. Institutions supported by the money of all persuasions, even though they be prisons, are not to be made schools for teaching Presbyterianism or Catholicism, Unitarianism or Methodism, Infidelity or Atheism, and this article says so. But this article goes no further. There is nothing in it that prohibits religion as distinguished from the particular creed or tenets of religious and anti-religious sects and denominations being taught anywhere.

That pure and undefiled religion which appertains to the relationship and responsibility of man to God, and is readily distinguishable from the creeds of sects ; that religion which permeates all our laws, which is recognized in every sentence against crime and immorality, which is invoked in every oath, which is reverentially deferred to every morning at that desk and on like occasions at the

4

Capitol of every State of the Union; that religion which is recognized by our Presidents and Governors every year in the thanksgivings of the people, to which one-seventh part of the century which has just closed has been devoted ; that reli-religion which is our history, which is our unwritten as well as our written law, and which sustains the pillars of our liberty, is a very, very different thing from the particular creeds or tenets of either religionists or infidels. And this article places no unhallowed touch upon that religion. While we punish the viola-tions of the oath or other moral obligation, it would be monstrous by affirmative legislation to restrict religious instruction. On this subject, let me briefly quote from Story and Webster and Washington. Story says :

"It is impossible for those who believe in the truth of Christianity as a divine revela-"tion to doubt that it is the especial duty of government to foster and encourage it among "all the citizens and subjects. This is a point wholly distinct from that of the right of "private judgment in matters of religion and of the freedom of public worship according "to the dictates of one's conscience."

Webster says :

"If we work upon marble, it will perish; if we work upon brass, time will efface it; if "we rear temples, they will crumble to the dust. But if we work on men's immortal "minds; if we imbue them with high principles, with the just fear of God and of their "fellow-men, we engrave on those tablets something which no time can efface, but "which will brighten and brighten to all eternity."

Washington, in his Farewell Address, says :

"Of all the dispositions and habits which lead to prosperity, religion and morality are "indispensable supports. In vain would that man claim the tribute of patriotism who "should labor to subvert these great pillars of human happiness, these purest props of the "duties of men and citizens. The mere politician equally with the pious man ought to "respect and cherish them A volume could not trace all their connections with private "and public felicity. Let it simply be asked where is the security for property, for rep-"utation, for life, if the sense of religious obligation desert the oaths which are the in-"struments of investigation in courts of justice? And let us with caution indulge the "supposition that morality can be maintained without religion. Whatever may be con-"ceded to the influence of refined education on minds of peculiar structure, reason and "experience both forbid us to expect that national morality can prevail in exclusion of "religious principle."

Again, some one has said that he thought the Bible was a religious book. That remark arises, sir, from a provision in the article of amendment that sectarian creeds are to be excluded, but that this provision shall not be construed to exclude the Bible. Let me say that the saving clause in favor of the Bible is just, because it is a religious and not a sectarian book.

I have a few words more to say. There is one provision in the article to which I have not called attention. If the amendment to the Constitution is to answer any purpose, it is to exclude sectarian teachings from public schools, and this article says so. That expression might be perverted to effect the exclusion of the Bible, and the provision that it shall not be so construed was necessary to exclude that conclusion, so as to leave the Bible in its relations to the public schools and institutions where it stands now.

It says that, while Shakespeare and Homer, Junius and Juvenal are not to be excluded, the Bible shall not, by reason of this article, be excluded. The Consti-tution of this country will never treat that book with disrespect. No party will ever have it tabooed. Who wants this article to exclude the Bible ?

Not the Catholics. It is the rule of their faith and practice and they want more, not less, religious instruction. They were the first in this country when establish-ing the government of Maryland to provide in her fundamental law for religious freedom. The Protestants do not want it excluded, because it is their rule of faith. The Israelite does not want it excluded, because it is a guide to his conscience. The atheist does not want it excluded, for he recognizes no superior ; he is a law unto himself. It is a matter of indifference to him whether the Bible or Dabold's Arithmetic or Hale's History of the United States is used in the school, so far as his conscience is concerned.

But then we are told that there are different translations of the Bible. True, and yet there is but one Bible ; that is the revelation from on High. There are vari-ous translations, and the excellence of this article is that it prevents the exclusion of any. Nothing in this article shall be construed to exclude either the Douay or the King James version. I am for the broadest toleration, but I would never agree to a constitutional amendment that would exclude from the schools the Bible. The Constitution should neither say that it should or should not be read in the schools. To attempt either would be to mingle politics with religion, which all would deprecate. Make the Bible a political ensign, and a party spirit such as clustered around the white and red roses would be aroused, in which perhaps there would be no more piety than there was in the spirit that animated Richard the Lion-hearted and his followers when they rallied around the Cross, or Saladin and his Mohammedan hordes when they fought for the Crescent.

Into such a conflict, having foresworn all idolatry, even though the Bible be on the shrine, I will not enter. " Put up thy sword, my kingdom is not of this world," is the injunction of our religion. But this article of the Constitution must not exclude it unless we come to the conclusion that the narrative of the creation, that the maxims of Solomon, that the logic of Paul, and those truths that have lighted up the future to unnumbered generations, are injurious to public morals.

Mr. President, where shall we go for public morals? If you must exclude the Bible you must banish all our literature or expurgate it, for it would be the height of folly to say that it is lawful to drink from the conduits which human hands had made, but not from the pure fountain. Where shall we go? To the Koran? To Confucius? To the Mormon book of their lord? To the vain philosophy of the ancients? To mythological fables? No, sir; the people of this country want that book let alone. The Constitution must not touch it. It is to be forced upon no one and the Constitution is to make it unlawful to read it nowhere.

RIVER AND HARBOR BILL.

The Senate, as in Committee of the Whole, resumed the consideration of the bill (H. R. No. 3022) making appropriations for the construction, repair, preservation, and completion of certain public works on rivers and harbors, and for other purposes—

Mr. FRELINGHUYSEN said :

Mr. President, I have just listened with pleasure to the constitutional doctrine applicable to this bill stated by the Senator from Kentucky, [Mr. STEVENSON,] and yet I shall probably not vote with him. I cannot vote for the amendment of the Senator from Vermont, [Mr. EDMUNDS,] which is to appropriate $4,000,000 and leave it to the administration of the Secretary of War. I do not think $4,000,000 is a sufficient appropriation. I shall not vote to re-commit the bill because the chairman of the committee, or the Senator having the bill in charge, has submitted to the Senate a substitute for the bill, which probably incorporates all the advantages we would derive from a re-committal, and I propose, when the opportunity comes, to vote for that substitute.

I confess that I feel more kindly toward this measure than some of those with whom I am in the habit of coinciding. If I believed that this country or nation was poor, I would move and vote to lay the bill on the table. I know that the country is not poor. The people are somewhat poor, and I am very sorry for it; and there need be no question as to what makes them so. If, in a circle a hundred miles in diameter on our prairies, you gather all the cereals produced in the land for five or six years and then drive in all the sheep and horses and oxen, and pile on all the fabrics and all the productions of a highly stimulated industry, and then gather around it the best youth of the country, with their energy and muscle and capacity to produce, and let them put the torch to that vast funeral pile and then leap into it themselves, no one would wonder that as the smoke from that destruction went up to propitiate the Moloch of war that there should be poverty in the land. Or if you stimulate every energy of a country so that it is fevered and excited and every nerve so strained that it is ready to break, it is certain that there

6

will be a reaction, an exhaustion, a prostration; and that is just what this country is now suffering.

The people are poor, but the country has vast hidden resources, and it seems to me that the way to make the people rich is by developing these resources; and I do not think that I am stating an extravagant proposition when I say that the only means of making the people rich is by developing those resources, for I do not know any other source from which we derive wealth and luxury but this rugged earth from whence we come and whither we go.

If I believed that this bill was to burden the people with taxes I would move and vote to lay it on the table; but I know it is not. The question whether we appropriate four million or five million is the question whether we shall next year pay one million more or less on the public debt, and that is all of it. I believe that by appropriating with reasonable liberality and developing the resources of the country we enable ourselves to pay five million five years hence much easier than we can pay one million next year.

Mr. President, it seems to me that we should learn something from the past. Look at the developments and at the increase of the wealth of the country in the last fifty years. I can remember when the good and patriotic men of the country feared that the nation was going to be ruined by its very increase and development; by the remoteness of its parts they feared that it would fall to pieces. Then it was that hidden in the earth was found the wealth of iron, which was followed by the introduction of railroads, binding the land together, and then by the invention of the telegraph, which has made the people of this vast continent one community, so that San Francisco is to-day for all practical purposes nearer, much nearer to the Atlantic seaboard than Cincinnati was then. Then I remember that reflecting men said we were to be ruined for the want of fuel, and then we found the illimitable fields of coal, supplying not only domestic purposes but the vastly greater demands of manufacturing and transportation. Then, as the New London whaler came in without any cargo, thoughtful men said we were to have an oil famine and that we would be straitened what to do in the numerous purposes to which it is applied; then some man in Pennsylvania drove a pipe down into the earth and developed a supply of oil, enough for the world. A great man has said of the world what is true of this country; he said that the world is God's hot-bed, that He has planted deep and multifariously, and there are many things which have not yet come up. The Senator from Wisconsin, [Mr. HOWE,] in a speech of a few minutes the other day, hit the very point when he said that it was the duty of the Government to water our country's crops and make the seed sprout.

But, Mr. President, besides all that, this is the proper time to make the appropriation. We have hitherto decided that these improvements are fit to be made and valuable, and we now can make one dollar of expenditure produce two dollars in the results of work, and the people want the occupation and the money. The Senator from Ohio [Mr. THURMAN] says that is making this Government parental. Well, if developing the wealth of the country, even if the people do thereby incidentally gain employment, if increasing the revenues of the nation is making the Government parental, let it be parental. There is much of wise political economy in the saying of Solomon: "There is that scattereth, and yet increaseth; and "there is that withholdeth more than is meet, but it tendeth to poverty."

Neither do I think that these appropriations should be confined to salt water or to deep water. I do not differ from the Senator from Kentucky as to the constitutional rule relative to internal improvements. The question which determines the propriety of an appropriation for an internal improvement is whether it will be for the general welfare. In the language of the Constitution, do "we lay the "taxes, duties, imposts, and excises in order to pay the debts and provide for the "common defense and general welfare of the United States?" If we do, we are acting in harmony with the Constitution. It is the eighth section of article one that gives us the constitutional power to make these appropriations, and the question suggested is the test as to whether any particular improvement comes within the purview of that section of the Constitution.

It may be that a stream three feet wide may float lumber and grain and coal so as to promote the general welfare of the United States, and if it does its improvement is within the legitimate powers of the Constitution. If it be waters entirely within one State confined in its benefits to a mere locality, it is a perversion of the Constitution to claim that the General Government is to spend money in its improvement. The provision of the Constitution relative to the regulation of commerce which has been so much discoursed upon has nothing to do with this question. Under that provision the Government can take control of all navigable waters, but under the general-welfare clause it can improve land or water without taking control of either.

Mr. President, one word more. Every dollar that we expend for these improvements probably stimulates twenty dollars from private capital, and thus increases the wealth and the revenues of the nation. Besides, there are many other reasons why individual States cannot so well make these improvements as the General Government. It is a little extraordinary, I know, that one State deriving no direct advantage should be taxed for an improvement in another State; thus, for instance, the State of New Jersey has little or no beneficial interest in this bill; she does not receive a fourth as much as she will contribute to the amount expended; but then, sir, we are one people, one nation; we all have a common interest, and I rejoice in any legislation which brings practically and vividly to the people of different sections the beneficent influences of this one great nation. Mr. President, we are rich enough, our history is sufficiently glorious, the prospects of the future are bright enough; there is but one thing we want, and that is for every section and every party to determine that the great provision of the Constitution enacting that all persons born or naturalized in the United States and subject to the jurisdiction thereof shall be citizens thereof and of the State in which they reside, shall everywhere be enforced so that every citizen, white and black, at the North and South, shall fully and freely enjoy full American citizenship, with the inalienable right to life, liberty, and the pursuit of happiness. If only that could be vouchsafed, this nation would this year enter upon a career most grand and glorious.

DIPLOMATIC AND CONSULAR BILL.

Mr. FRELINGHUYSEN said:

Mr. President, I move that the Senate further insists on its amendments to the diplomatic and consular appropriation bill, and that a committee of conference be granted as asked by the House of Representatives; and, in view of some remarks which have been made elsewhere in reference to that bill, I wish to say a few words.

The diplomatic service was organized and the salaries fixed in 1856 under Mr. Pierce's administration. The purchasing power of a dollar then was certainly a third more than it is now. Since that time there has been an increase in salaries of about $50,000, that sum being compensated, as I understand it, by the price which has been demanded for passports, being $5 for each individual. The House of Representatives made extensive changes in this bill, in the countries to which we should send representatives, and in the amount of salaries to be paid. The Committee on Appropriations referred the bill to the Committee on Foreign Relations. They appointed a sub-committee, and that sub-committee met the Committee on Appropriations and without regard to their political views advised them that no change in existing laws should be made. Consequently, the Committee on Appropriations did not agree to the change of the law, but reported the bill to the Senate with amendments retaining the law as it then and now existed, and with great unanimity the Senate passed the bill with the amendments. The House, as they had a right, still insisted upon this change in the laws.

Mr. President, these existing salaries are moderate. They are such as are required to enable any person to live in republican respectability. They cannot be made less without rendering these positions mere decorations of millionaires.

This disagreement between the two Houses led to a conference. I am not aware that there was anything then said in reference to changing the law. The conferees on the part of the Senate hoped to bring the conferees on the part of the House to their views. Failing in that, the conferees of the Senate then offered to divide the difference between the amount of salaries fixed by the House and those provided by existing laws and insisted on by the Senate. That offer was rejected. Another conference was called. The conferees on the part of the Senate proposed then, for the sake of coming to a settlement, to adopt the appropriation as made by the House, and that the President, as was the case in the earlier days of the Republic, should have the distribution, the administration of this fund ; providing further that he should not apply any of this fund to pay a diplomat at any official post which did not exist under the present laws, and providing also that no salary should be increased, and providing further that a committee should be appointed, consisting of two members of each House, who should adjust these salaries, and that every person holding office in the diplomatic and consular service should be subject, in his salary, to such legislation as might be adopted on that report at the next session of Congress. Had this offer been accepted there would probably have been no difficulty, no question would have arisen ; for the President in the exercise of his good judgment would doubtless have discontinued the less important diplomatic positions and paid the full salary to those which could not be dispensed with.

That offer was rejected by the House, they insisting that in addition the conferees on the part of the Senate should agree that there should be no claim for any salary beyond the amount thus appropriated. In other words, they called upon us as conferees to change the law which both Houses had established, and this we were to do to prevent the appropriations from failing. Well, Mr. President, for one—and I do not want to say anything indiscreet—I would let that appropriation bill fail and every other before I would legislate upon such terms.

Legislation upon appropriations bills is a bad practice, but it has precedent. It is a bad practice, for the reason that our Constitution creates three negatives on the passage of every law. The House has a negative on the Senate, the Senate has a negative on the House, the President has a negative on both. This legislation on appropriation bills virtually deprives the President of his negative. But that was not the question before the committee.

The question was whether the Senate at the close of a session should be driven to such legislation as they did not approve, as they had with great unanimity declared against, for fear that the appropriation bill should fail. I do not like to legislate under any fear, and my opinion is that the Senate does not. I deprecate this difference between the two Houses ; but the Senate cannot do otherwise than to decline to accede to the claim that is made by the other House. That claim strikes at the very corner-stone of the Government. The first article of the Constitution declares that the legislative power shall be vested in the Congress, consisting of a Senate and of a House of Representatives. All civilized governments recognize the wisdom of having two branches of the legislature ; every State of the Union has endorsed the policy of this form of government.

When our Constitution was formed an important compromise was made to preserve the popular feature of our Government. To prevent the States from having an undue power in matters of taxation, so as to prevent Rhode Island and Delaware and New Jersey having a voice in taxation equal to New York and Virginia, it was provided that all bills for raising revenue should originate with the House of Representatives, the Senate having the right to propose and concur in amendments, as in other cases. This, according to my view, does not confer on the House the right to originate appropriation bills ; but precedent, which makes law, which aggregates to itself power, is in favor of this claim by the House. I do not care now to dispute that position ; but let us be careful how we make further precedents. The conferees of the Senate on this bill not only did not question the right of the House to originate the bill, but surrendered all the Senate amendments, and agreed to take just the sum that the House appropriated ; but we were told that we must go further, and change existing laws. Thus while the Senate gives the House the fullest benefit of the great compromise, the House demands that the States as represented in the Senate shall be silenced not only on appropriation bills but on general legislation. The Senate is told in relation to this and other bills that it must alter the law naming the countries to which we send representatives, that we must alter the law fixing the salaries, to all of which the House has agreed ; that we must alter the law organizing the Army ; that we must reduce the Army from 25,000 to 11,000 ; that we must change our Indian policy ; that we must repeal our registry and election laws, and such like legislation.

Now, Mr. President, the Senate cannot agree to this demand of the House, because it would be destructive of the most fundamental principle of the Government, which is, that the legislative power of the United States shall be vested in a Congress which shall consist of a Senate and House of Representatives. We cannot agree to it, because it would be violating the very compromise of the Constitution under which the House claims its right to originate money bills ; the consideration for agreeing to that was the States should have their voice on all legislation in the Senate.

To agree to the demand of the House would be the most objectionable centralization and destructive of the rights of the States, if the Senate is to be brought at the end of a session to accede to just such legislation as is demanded of us or else the appropriations must all fail.

Further, to agree to the demand of the House would be to destroy that stability of the Government which is derived from the existence of the constitutional powers of the Senate. In order to give that stability the term of a Senator continues through three Congresses, only one-third of the Senators going out every two years. But where is the stability if at the close of any session we are to be brought to adopt just such legislation as one branch of Congress demands of us ? The Senate might just as well have no legislative power as to have legislative power only when we are suffered to exercise it.

I have been surprised in looking at the RECORD at some remarks made by a Senator for whose judgment and unpartisan patriotism I have much respect, to which I must make an allusion. The Senator said :

" I say that upon the high responsibility of their oaths and their duty to the country, " it might be, although not likely to be, that the House or the Senate would be justified " in saying, 'Reduce the Army one-half, reduce the Navy one-half, or take the alterna- " tive of no Army or no Navy at all.' "

Mr. President, a law, which the Senate and every member of it, the House of Representatives and every member, are just as much bound to respect as the wayfaring man, declares that the Army of the United States shall consist of twenty-five thousand men ; and we are told that the House of Representatives or the Senate, separately, have on their oaths and on their responsibility to the country the right to say that that Army shall be reduced to twelve thousand. Well, if the House or Senate has the right to say that the Army shall be reduced to twelve thousand, either has the right to say that it shall be reduced to nine thousand, and if to nine, to six, and if to six, it may be abolished. They have the same right, and it is so claimed, in regard to the Navy, and if either House acting separately can reduce the Navy one-half, it can, on their oaths and their responsibilities to the country, abolish it entirely. So either House can determine that the Executive shall receive but one-half of the compensation fixed by law, and that no greater appropriation shall be made, and if so, can say that no appropriation shall be made for the Executive. So, too, either House may say that the Supreme Court shall consist of but three instead of nine justices and make their appropriations accordingly. So the House may say that the Senate shall have but half the appropriation required by law for the salaries of Senators, and, if but half, it may say there shall be no appropriation, and thus abolish it. Mr. President, that will not do. The Senate and the House of Representatives are bound by their oaths, by their responsibilities to the country, to make the appropriations that are necessary to carry out existing laws. The Senate and the House of Representatives have no right to make appropriations for any other purpose than to carry out existing laws. Appropriations are incident to existing laws, and may not be used as an instrumentality to coerce legislation.

Mr. President, this nation has in our generation passed through a fearful ordeal.

2

Five hundred thousand brave men, North and South, have died in that great trial but our Republic, as it was given to us by our fathers, we possess intact. The Executive performs his functions; the judiciary discharges its duties; the Representatives of a free people at the other end of the Capitol legislate like freemen. This Senate hitherto has legislated freely and untrammeled; and will, sir, I trust, forever continue so to do.

I hope that a better spirit will prevail, and that all will see that not because the Senate will not, but because it cannot, it declines to be placed in any position where it cannot legislate freely.

DEATH OF SENATOR O. S. FERRY.

Mr. FRELINGHUYSEN said:

Mr. President, change is written on everything with which we are familiar. The spring, the summer, the golden autumn, and the icy winter chase each other, and while we recognize the one it is gone. The forest is no sooner clothed in its luxuriant foliage than it begins to disrobe, and presently its bare poles stand up against the sky. The creations of human industry and genius, whether of kingdom or code, of monument or picture, crumble away before this universal law. These changes are fraught with instruction, and remind us that we shall not long continue as we now are. But it is when the stern messenger calls away a companion distinguished for his genius and his eloquence, his purity and his Christian faith, that we learn the most impressive of moral lessons.

The average age of the members of this body is perhaps fifty years. In that past period a thousand, yes, nearer two thousand, millions of sentient beings such as we, capable of indefinite if not of infinite moral and intellectual development, have appeared upon the stage of time, there rejoiced and emulated, suffered and striven, and have then departed forever; their entry and their exit being alike mysterious.

Brief as has been their visit to earth, it has been long enough to effect several demonstrations:

It has proven that there is a spiritual as well as a material existence; for they were all conscious of being, and they were all recognized as being, in their personality, spiritual.

It has proven that they were moral intelligences, for no matter how enfeebled by want or how degraded by bad associations, there never was one of that mighty host, with every selfish inducement to decide in his own favor, who has not condemned and blamed himself for every wrong he committed.

It has proven, by the acquisitions those intelligences have made in languages and laws, in philosophy and art, that they are capable of perpetual progression.

It has proven that they were not the results of natural causes, for they have seized upon nature and made it subservient to their pleasure. The very elements have been subjected to their service; its obstacles, such as oceans and space, storms and lightnings, have been overcome and conquered.

Our race stands out the supernatural by an irrefragable logic. If this be not true, why admire the heroism of the martyr dying for his faith more than the fire that consumes him? Why render more homage to the patriot soldier who dies in front of the line than to the steed which spur and bridle have forced to the danger? Why more gratitude to a friendship that is true amid temptations to betray than to the steady current of the river that makes its way over rocks and precipices? It is man as a positive force superior to nature that we admire.

In him we to-day lament the intellectual and moral was in a marked degree predominant. His physical infirmities seemed to augment that supremacy. In the prime of life, shattered by disease, he resolutely and firmly adjusted himself to the situation. We have seen him standing there, advocating those measures he believed best for his country, while his countenance was distorted from pain. His spirit firmly held the mastery over physical forces. They could not carry the citadel of his soul.

He had, too, marked independence of character and thought, and possessed the concomitant virtue of courage. He was satisfied of his ability by investigation to arrive at a sound conclusion. He knew that his motives were pure and honest, and when his opinions were formed he was not to be swerved from them. Though not indifferent to popular opinion, as no sound mind is, he had much of the spirit of that old hero who said : " Were there as many devils in Worms as roof-tiles, I would on."

I did not always think him right, but I always felt re-assured where I found myself voting as he voted.

He was a man of good education and attainments. He had not high culture ; few men have. High culture is not essential to excellence or usefulness ; if it were, our republican institutions, State and national, would be in a sad condition. His education was sufficient to have developed his native powers and to render him conscious of his strength, so that he went fearlessly and successfully forward as a leader in life's duties.

Mr. FERRY'S reasoning powers were of a superior order, and were habitually fortified by careful reflection on the subject he would present. He seized the strong point of the question under investigation and wielded it with great power. In presenting his views he was direct, plain, and logical, and in that he impressed his hearers with the strength of his own convictions, so that they sympathized with him. He was eloquent.

When that terrible calamity, the record of which is found in thousands of desolate homes, overtook our country, his patriotism shone forth. A Representative of the nation, he became a patrol to guard its capital ; and afterward, at the head of the Fifth Connecticut Cavalry, bravely participated in its battles. But his patriotism was not sectional ; it was not a narrow sentiment, confined to any locality. He fought to preserve here for all his country that civil liberty which, while the greatest of blessings, is conferred upon only a few spots of earth. He believed that he was contending for the right. I do not say he would not say that many of those with whom he contended did not, from their standpoint, think they were right ; but this is true : when everywhere in this free Republic law shall be supreme, the rights of property and person secure, and constitutional political equality exercised and protected ; then, when civil liberty is thus established, and we rejoice in the prosperity, peace, and virtue that flow from it, all will remember past differences only to be the more grateful that we are again friends.

It was the crowning glory of our friend that he was a Christian. Conscious of a spiritual malady which human culture or educational development could not cure, he sought and found for a disease to the supernatural a supernatural remedy.

He has gone from us forever. Whither has he gone? All of him that is mortal quietly reposes in the soil of the gallant State that delighted to honor him—his memory is embalmed in the hearts of many loving countrymen—and his spirit has returned to the bosom of his Father.

INDIAN APPROPRIATION BILL.

The Senate resumed the consideration of the bill (H. R. No. 3478) making appropriations for the current and contingent expenses of the Indian Department, and for fulfilling treaty stipulations with various Indian tribes for the year ending June 30, 1877, and for other purposes—

Mr. FRELINGHUYSEN said :

Mr. President, I do not rise to make a speech, but cannot avoid expressing my disapprobation of this measure to transfer the Indians of the country to the charge of the War Department. I am glad that Senators have given the attention to this subject that they have, and have made such able expositions of the subject that the country may fully understand the measure.

Mr. President, in our interior and on our frontier there is a people which every Senator knows and the civilized world knows we are bound by every obligation of justice, of humanity, and of honor to protect and cherish as our wards. Once they were rich and we were poor; they were free and we dependent; they were powerful and we were weak; and there is not a generous heart in America that does not to-day regret that our prosperity has been disastrous to them. There is a remnant of that people still with us, toward whom we have the opportunity of making some indemnity for the wrong that we have done those whom we have superseded. There is a remnant toward whom we by our justice and by our generosity can relieve somewhat the national conscience and do something to improve the reputation of our country. Within the last few years we have seen measures taken to that end. Every religious denomination of the country—the Methodists, the Presbyterians, the Catholics, and the Episcopalians—has joined with the Chief Magistrate, as distinguished for his humanity as for his courage, and has been vigorously at work to ameliorate the condition of the Indians. These denominations contribute their money, they send their missionaries, they select the Indian agent, and in many instances he is the agent of his denomination in distributing their benefactions. The religious community of the country feel the deepest interest in this subject. They ask no change. The chairman of the Committee on Indian Affairs assures me that every religious denomination in the country asks that things may remain as they are—the Indians without exception ask that they may remain as they are—the President of the United States, who has this subject at heart, asks that things may remain as they are—and yet we propose with a ruthless hand to break down this noble work of charity and justice, and, while all are satisfied, propose to hand this whole subject over to the War Department.

I should like to know in what capacity it is that the War Department is to take charge of the Indians. Does the Senate of the United States undertake to say that it will in times of peace render inhabitants of this country subject militarily to the War Department? Are we to take 55,000 civilized inhabitants of this country, and all other Indians, and say "you shall be subject to the sword?" I presume that nobody will assume that we intend any such thing; and I do not understand the advocates of this measure to place it upon that ground. If I am mistaken I should like to be corrected. As no one so asserts, I assume that the advocates of this measure hold that these Indians are not to be subject to the soldiers and officers of the Army in a military capacity; that would be an atrocity that no one would advocate.

You cannot send the military into any part of the country where there is insurrection, even at the call of the governor, such is the jealousy of our people, that there is not an outcry against the supremacy of the military power over the civil power.

Well, if the officers and soldiers of the Army do not take charge of this subject in a military capacity, I should like to know what advantage is to accrue from the proposed change to the border States, who say that this subject is more interesting in its effects to them than upon those States that are remote from the Indian tribes. They can receive no more protection from the Army after the transfer than they do now.

But, Mr. President, if the Indian Bureau is not transferred to the War Department in its military capacity, I should like to know by what authority we can transfer the civil administration of this country to the Army. What right have we to transfer the administration of any civil interests of the nation to the Army? It is a violation of the very spirit of the Constitution. The Indian agents are civil officers; their functions are civil; they are nominated by the President and confirmed by the Senate. The Constitution requires that these officers shall so be created. But this bill undertakes to say that the Congress of the United States shall confer the functions of these civil officers upon the Army, thus in effect usurping the power of the President by nomination and the power of the Senate by confirmation to select the persons who shall perform those civil duties.

Mr. President, this should not be a political question, and I hope that the Senate of the United States will show the American people that they are prepared to do justice to this afflicted race, and that the people will have the support and countenance of the Senate in their work of justice and charity, and I hope that this step in retrogression, this step which seems to be more an advance toward barbarism than toward civilization, will not, in this year of our Lord 1876, receive the approval of the American Senate.

IMPEACHMENT OF WILLIAM W. BELKNAP.

The Senate sitting as a court of impeachment for the trial of William W. Belknap, late Secretary of War, and having under consideration the question of jurisdiction—

MR. FRELINGHUYSEN said.

Mr. President: I will first call attention to a consideration which has been much pressed upon the Senate, but which is not involved in the question before us, namely : Whether an officer can resign after he is impeached and thus oust jurisdiction.

I will, secondly, consider the true question we are to decide, namely : Have we jurisdiction in this case?

I. The Senate is not called upon to decide whether the resignation of a civil officer after articles of impeachment have been presented against him ousts the jurisdiction of the Senate and deprives it of the power to try the impeachment. That case is not before us. William W. Belknap had resigned the office of Secretary of War, and his resignation had been duly accepted, before the House of Representatives impeached him. The suggestion that, inasmuch as the resignation and the impeachment were made on the same day, the law will not take notice of the fact that the resignation was in point of time prior to the impeachment, because the law ignores fractions of days, is unsound. The law does observe fractions of days, whenever any right depends upon its doing so. The law never causes or suffers a citizen to suffer anything by a fiction. Abundant authority and examples to sustain this position could be adduced were it necessary.

But if the question was whether Belknap could have avoided the jurisdiction of the Senate by resigning his office after he had been impeached by the House, much might be said against such a claim. As that question is not before the Senate, I will give no opinion on it. Were it here, it might be argued thus :

It is essential to every investigation that there be some point of time to which the tribunal shall direct its inquiries as to the truth of the facts alleged. That point of time in civil actions is the service of the original process ; in criminal proceedings it is the finding of the indictment ; and in proceedings for the judgment of impeachment, it is the time of the impeachment by the House. If the action be to eject from lands, the abandoning or vacating the possession of the land after the process is served cannot be pleaded with effect in bar of the suit ; but the suit proceeds to a judgment of eviction and for mesne profits and costs as if possession had been retained. If the action is for a nuisance, the judgment is that the nuisance be abated, even although the nuisance was removed immediately after the suit was commenced. If the judgment be for damages for neglecting some duty, such as the execution of an instrument, performance after the suit has been commenced cannot be pleaded with effect as a bar to the action. If the proceeding be by indictment, say against an accessory, the State cannot sustain its charge by proving that defendant, after indictment found, aided the principal to escape. That fact, at most, could only be proven as persuasive evidence of the substantive fact averred in the indictment. In no legal proceeding will any act of the defendant after the suit is commenced, even though it should be the performance of the very thing sought by the suit, be a bar to the action, unless it be accepted by the party who of right is enforcing the duty.

If the House of Representatives had the right to impeach when they presented their articles, and thus commenced proceedings, the act of the respondent or of the President could not be pleaded as a bar to the proceeding. Neither can it be said, if the House had the right to impeach at the time they presented the articles, that it is absurd or incongruous that the judgment of removal from office, which under the Constitution must be pronounced on conviction, should be entered against one who, since the articles were so presented, has resigned the office. The right of the House to that judgment existed, if at all, when the proceedings were properly commenced, and all action of the respondent subsequent thereto is, in the eye of the law, as in all like cases, ignored. The House stands before the Senate with all the rights that other suitors have before other courts. Every affirmative judgment in civil or criminal proceedings is a mere judicial declaration of the existence of the right of the actor in the suit to be sustained and assured in the claim made when the legal proceedings were commenced. Where, I ask, would be the incongruity of a judgment of the Senate, were it customary to make up a judgment-roll, which should, in substance, read thus:

" William W. Belknap having, on the 2d of March, 1876, been impeached by
" the House of Representatives for high crimes, and the Senate having, on the
" demand of the House, proceeded to try the truth of the several articles of impeach-
" ment so presented, the Senate do, on this —— day of ——, 1876, adjudge that
" the said articles are sustained, and do pronounce, as their judgment, that the said
" William W. Belknap be removed from office, and that he be perpetually disquali-
" fied from holding any office of honor, trust, or profit under the United States."

There would be no incongruity between the judgment and the record, even though it appear that between the time the proceedings by the House were commenced and the rendition of the judgment William W. Belknap had resigned his office. He, by the hypothesis, was an officer when impeached by the House. The evidence had extended to that point of time and not beyond it. Was he, then, guilty had been the question throughout, and the judgment of the Senate in sustaining the claim of the House, speaks as of the day the proceedings were commenced. Such a judgment would be no more incongruous than that of a court which, having ascertained that a defendant was in possession of lands when the ejectment was commenced, and that the right of possession was then in the plaintiff, pronounced a judgment that the plaintiff recover, notwithstanding the defendant may have pleaded that he had abandoned the possession. Such a judgment would be no more incongruous than a judgment of six cents and costs against a defendant who, having at the time suit was commenced made default in the execution of an instrument it was his duty to have executed, should make it appear that he did execute it the day after process was served.

It might, in fact, be claimed that the argument in favor of the right of the House to retain jurisdiction, notwithstanding a resignation after the impeachment proceedings were commenced, was much stronger than in the cases supposed. The right of the House is to retain jurisdiction to satisfy their double demand, to wit, that the officer be removed, and that he also be disqualified. It would be a strange ruling which should hold that when jurisdiction had vested by the proceedings being commenced while the official was in office, it was divested by his complying with only half of the demand of the actor in the proceedings, to wit, "removal " from office," while the demand for " disqualification " is entirely unsatisfied and forever defeated, because the Constitution only authorizes a judgment of disqualification as an incident to, and as coupled with, a judgment of removal.

If the jurisdiction of the court depended on the parties, plaintiff and defendant, being residents of different States, the fact that the defendant the day after suit was commenced became a resident of the same State in which the plaintiff resided, would not affect the jurisdiction. When the jurisdiction of a Federal court depends on the fact that one of several defendants resides in a different State from that in which the plaintiff resides, the death of that defendant does not oust the court of jurisdiction. When jurisdiction has attached, it continues to the end. Jurisdiction attaches, if at all, under and by reason of the circumstances that exist when the proceedings are commenced, and no subsequent act but such as extinguishes the claim or abates the suit can divest that jurisdiction. And a judgment which is in harmony with the facts and conditions which exist at the time the proceedings are commenced cannot be called incongruous. Justice Story, who, as we shall see, holds that an officer cannot be impeached except while he is in office, gives no effect on the question of jurisdiction to his resignation after he is impeached. He says: "If, then, there must be a judgment of removal from " office, it would seem to follow that the Constitution contemplated that the party " was still in office *at the time of the impeachment*." (2 Story on the Constitution, § 801.) And by military law, while one who, by reason of his term of enlistment having expired, is entitled to his discharge from the service is not afterward subject to a court-martial, yet if proceedings are commenced against him before he is so entitled to his discharge they continue after his term of enlistment expires. (De Hart's Military Law, page 35.) I do not mean to say, however, that resignation of office or its termination by lapse of time while proceedings are pending may not, either upon a plea of *puis darrein continuance*, or a mere suggestion on the record, be specially recited in the judgment so as to correspond with the facts of the case. This would not interfere with the jurisdiction of the court to pronounce the constitutional judgment of removal and disqualification. Nor do I mean to say that the judgment would relate to the time of impeachment to such an extent as to render void the official acts of the officer while proceedings for impeachment were pending. The *actual* removal from office is only affected by conviction and judgment.

But, as before said, on the question whether one who is impeached by the House while in office can divest the jurisdiction of the Senate by resignation it is not necessary to give an opinion, because that is not before us. It is clear that much is to be said when that case arises. Enough has been said to show that it is very different from the question whether the House can impeach and whether the Senate have jurisdiction over one who at the time of the impeachment had ceased to be a civil officer.

And in determining the true question before us we need not be influenced by the equivocal and undignified position the two branches of the legislative department of the Government would find themselves in if, after the presentation of articles, after a protracted trial, and after deliberate consultation, and when the Senate was just about to pronounce its judgment, the accused could thwart the whole proceedings by a summary resignation. This consideration, presented to our sense of judicial propriety so frequently and with so much address by the managers, does not belong to this case. When the question of the effect of a resignation made after impeachment arises, it will be decided.

We have now to do with the effect of a resignation, not after, but before an impeachment by the House.

II. Has the Senate sitting as a court of impeachment jurisdiction to try a citizen whom the House of Representatives claim to have impeached, such impeachment by the House being made when he had ceased to be a civil officer ?

The procedure by impeachment was imported into our Constitution from the common parliamentary law of England, but it was placed there clipped and pruned of very many of its baneful incidents. Impeachment, associated with bills of attainder and of pains and penalties and *ex post facto* laws, was made in Great Britain an instrument of political persecution and partisan aggrandizement. It was through those agencies that the grossest injustice was perpetrated in the name of law; that men of political power were destroyed: that families of influence were blotted out, and that their estates were confiscated to become a reward to those who persecuted those who owned them.

Bills of attainder, which term includes bills of pains and penalties (1 Story on the Constitution, § 1344 ; Cummings *vs.* State of Missouri, 4 Wallace, 323) were sometimes directed against whole classes of people without naming the individuals. They were sentences pronounced by the legislative instead of the judicial branch of the government. They were often pronounced without evidence, on the surmise

16

or on the clamor, as the old books term it, of the Commons. The investigation, if any, was in the absence of the accused, without his having counsel, and without any recognition of the rules of evidence. The punishment, which was often the deprivation of estate, of inheritable blood, and of life, was determined by no pre-existing law.

Ex post facto laws imposed punishments for acts which were innocent at the time they were performed, or greatly changed and increased the punishments after the act was done.

Impeachments extended to others than officers of the government and to acts that no law had declared criminal. And without counsel, witnesses or jury, a mere majority of the Lords often pronounced the judgment of banishment and often of death against the accused.

Justice Miller, in speaking of the manner in which the framers of the Constitution regarded bills of attainder and of pains and penalties and *ex post facto* laws, says:

"It is no cause of wonder that men who had just passed successfully through a desperate struggle in behalf of civil liberty should feel a detestation for legislation of which these are prominent features." (*Ex parte* Garland, 4 Wallace, page 388.)

And Justice Story, in speaking of the men who framed the Constitution and modified the English procedure by *impeachment*, says:

"History had sufficiently admonished them that the power of impeachment had been thus mischievously and inordinately applied in other ages; and it was not safe to disregard those lessons which it had left for our instruction written not unfrequently in blood."

He then refers to cases where the final overthrow and capital execution of the accused was the result of political resentment. (Story on the Constitution, § 784.)

England had no written constitution, and Parliament was omnipotent; and each political party, as it rose to power, made use of this machinery of attainder, pains and penalties, *ex post facto* laws, and impeachments to oppress and weaken the rival party. The fathers of our Republic, familiar with the history of England, to escape these atrocities perpetrated in the name of law, determined that this nation *should have* a written constitution. They determined that the National Legislature should *not be* omnipotent, but that it should only possess delegated powers, reserving expressly to the States and to the people all other powers. So careful were they on this point that they even provided that the enumeration in the Constitution of the rights which belonged to the people should not be construed to deny or disparage such rights as were not enumerated in the Constitution.

As to these legalized agencies of tyranny, the framers of the Constitution provided, by article I, section 9, that Congress should not, and by section 10, that the States should not, pass any bills of attainder, and this includes bills of pains and penalties. And, as those provisions did not reach the judiciary, they provided, by article 3, section 3, that no attainder of treason should work a forfeiture except during the life of the person attainted. As to *ex post facto* laws, they prohibited their passage both to Congress and to the States.

And what did they provide as to the *procedure by impeachment?* They omitted to abolish or prohibit it, simply because that instrumentality was indispensable to a well-organized government. A President might be convicted of manslaughter, but that would not divest him of the presidential office. The Secretary of the Treasury might be sentenced for the crime of bribery, but he still might remain Secretary of the Treasury. The sentence of a judicial tribunal would not necessarily deprive any civil officer of his office. It was not desirable that the political power of removing from office should be given to the judiciary. Therefore, just as the House and the Senate were, by the Constitution, possessed with the right, by a two-thirds vote, to expel any member, so any civil officer, under greater restrictions than those incident to the expulsion of Members of Congress, might, on impeachment, by a two-thirds vote of the Senate, be removed from office. It is clear that but for this necessity the procedure by impeachment would never have been found in the Constitution.

The framers of the Constitution, however, in placing even the limited powers of impeachment in the Constitution were careful to divest it of its historic powers for oppression and tyranny. Let us be careful not to destroy the guards our fathers placed around this power.

They first provided that the House of Representatives should have the *sole* power of impeachment. It is provided that the House alone shall have the sole power to impeach, because there are cases where the Commons and the Lords joined in the impeachment and then the Lords tried the articles. (Selden's Judicature of Parliament, page 38.) So gross an outrage on justice as that of making the accuser and the judge identical it was determined to forbid by the provision that the House should have the *sole* power to impeach. And it is strange, indeed, that these words, inserted for so plain and salutary a purpose, should have been, as they have been, wrested from their purpose, and are claimed to have the effect of importing into the Constitution the whole common parliamentary law of Great Britain relative to impeachment, and that, by force of this provision, persons not civil officers are subject to impeachment by the House, and that the Senate are to try those whom the House may impeach, and that this impeachment extends to military as well as civil officers, and to the citizen as well as to the officer.

If any one considers these words so pregnant with meaning his opinion will probably be reversed as we proceed very briefly to consider the provisions of the Constitution.

They also provided that the Senate should have the *sole* power to try impeachments. This provision was inserted for a like reason as the former. Bills of attainder and pains and penalties, which were legislative conviction, were the work of both Houses of Parliament. And there are cases where the House had even assumed to convict on impeachment. And it was intended that it should be clearly understood that the Senate alone, in a judicial and not legislative capacity, was to try the charges which the House alone could make.

In England every description of person of both sexes were subject to impeachment. As the object in retaining the procedure in the Constitution was the removal from office, the Constitution restricted impeachment in its exercise to the President, Vice-President, and all civil officers "of the United States." I say restricted the power to those named, because, as the powers of the Constitution are delegated and limited, they can extend no further than is expressed. Unless the provision of the Constitution which declares that "the House of Representa-" tives shall have the sole power of impeachment" imports into the Constitution the entire power of impeachment as it existed under the common parliamentary law of England, it is certainly true that the fourth section of the second article, providing that "the President, Vice-President, and all civil officers of the United "States shall be removed from office on impeachment for and conviction of "treason, bribery, or other high crimes and misdemeanors," has the same signifi-cance as if it stated that no one, excepting the President, Vice-President, and all other civil officers of the United States, shall be liable to impeachment. A per-son who has duly resigned his civil office before any jurisdiction in impeachment has attached is no more a civil officer than he was before he entered upon the office.

The purpose of the framers of the Constitution was specifically to define who should be subject to impeachment, so as, in view of the scope of impeachment in England, to exclude those they intended should not be so subject. Had they in-tended to subject to impeachment not only those in office, but the larger number of those who ever have been, they would have said so. At all events it is true, according to the established rule of construing a penal provision, that it must be so said before we can by any authority hold that an unmentioned class are subject criminally. Persons not in civil office are not civil officers, and so do not come within the *descriptio personæ* of the Constitution.

In harmony with the provision that only persons in office at the time they are impeached are liable to impeachment is the mandatory provision of the Constitu-tion that the President and Vice-President and all civil officers *shall*, on impeach-ment and conviction of the crimes named, be *removed from* office.

Nothing can be more incongruous than that a person who is in no office at the time the House impeaches, which is the time to which the judgment must relate,

3

and when the jurisdiction attaches, should be subject to a judgment that he be removed from office.

In still further harmony with the provision that only those in office can be impeached is the provision that judgment in cases of impeachment shall not extend further than removal from office and disqualification to hold or enjoy any office of honor, trust, or profit under the United States. This provision is introduced in view of the past history of impeachment, where forfeiture, banishment, and death were not unfrequently imposed. The provisions of the Constitution relative to the judgment that may be rendered, taken together, amount to this : The judgment shall be removal from office or removal from office and disqualification.

The judgment of disqualification cannot be severed from that of removal any more than a judge can pronounce as a sentence a less penalty than the minimum prescribed. So both the judgment for removal and the judgment of disqualification require that the person proceeded against be in office when the impeachment is made by the House, to which point of time the judgment relates.

I do not see how the Constitution could more plainly have stated that it intended to circumscribe the ancient procedure by impeachment and intended that under our system it should be restricted to those in office when impeached than by saying in effect, first, that it should be restricted to the President, Vice President, and all civil officers, (for that is what it does say, inasmuch as those words are found in a constitution of delegated powers,) and by secondly saying that the judgment in impeachment shall be removal from office or removal from office and disqualification.

Again, if impeachment is applicable to those not in office, it must be so applicable as a means of imposing punishment for offenses committed while in office.

But this cannot be so, because the exclusive province of impeachment, as found in our Constitution, is the protection of civil office from vicious men. The judgment must be removal, and, as an incident thereto, may be disqualification. The object of impeachment is in no legal sense punishment. Removal from office and disqualification inflict mortification and suffering ; but this is in no true sense punishment ; it is rather an incident to than the object of the judgment. The pains thus inflicted are always less severe the more abandoned and vicious is the subject of it, and this is the reverse of the rule upon which punishment is imposed.

The greatest abuse of this procedure in England arose from making punishment the end of impeachment ; and hence it is that the Constitution contains the prohibition against any further judgment than removal and disqualification, and, to show that punishment is not the object of the Constitution in that connection, it immediately adds :

"But the party convicted shall nevertheless be liable and subject to indictment, "trial, judgment, and punishment, according to law."

To claim that the object of impeachment is punishment is to claim that the Constitution is inconsistent with itself.

If disqualification is a punishment, it is an infamous punishment ; and, if so, the offense for which it is imposed is infamous ; for the character of the punishment is always held to classify the crime. But the Constitution provides (5th amendment) that no person shall be held to answer for an infamous crime unless on a presentation or indictment of a grand jury. Here is no such indictment, and yet there is, in fact, no inconsistency in the Constitution, because this procedure is not to punish crime ; it is to protect the civil offices of the nation. It makes other provision for the punishment of crime, so as not to be misunderstood.

Again, it is contrary to natural justice and to the expressed spirit, if not letter, of the Constitution, and contrary to the common law, that one should be twice punished for the same offense, because the law in each case demands full expiation ; but here it is claimed that one is to be punished by the Senate, and then, by the express provision of the Constitution, is to be fully punished in the courts. We impose no punishments ; we simply protect the offices of the Republic from bad men.

Again, the Constitution provides that in all criminal prosecutions the accused shall have a trial by jury, and shall have such trial in the district where the crime was committed. If the proceeding by impeachment is for punishment, it is for the punishment of a crime, and hence comes within the provision of the Constitution which extends to "all criminal prosecutions," and the accused would be entitled to a jury, which is denied him.

There are two criminals before us convicted on impeachments: one is convicted of a treason that has shaken the pillars of the Republic and decimated the land by death; the other is a poor postmaster, who under temptation has appropriated a few stamps; and we are to impose the punishment, and we sentence each to removal from office and disqualification. The claim that our judgment is in any legal sense punishment seems to me an absurdity.

But if the object of the procedure by impeachment is not punishment, what is it that gives us jurisdiction over one out of office? It is not to remove from office, for that is an impossibility. It is not to pronounce a judgment of disqualification, for that the Constitution tells us only extends to one who is a civil officer, and also tells us that the judgment of disqualification must be coupled with a judgment of removal. We have no more authority to pronounce a separate judgment of disqualification than would a judge have to impose a penalty of only $50 for larceny when the statute said the penalty should be twenty days' imprisonment and $50 fine.

No express provision can be found in the Constitution extending impeachment by the House to those who are *not*, but have been, civil officers, unless, as before stated, the provision that the House shall have the *sole* power of impeachment imports the whole English system with all its atrocities into our Government. Not only so, but the express provisions of a Constitution conferring limited powers negative such a claim.

If impeachment can be extended to those who have been in office it must be by implication, by inference, and because incident to some power that is conferred, and because of its marked propriety.

Can any one believe that the framers of the Constitution, with the history of impeachment and its associate legal instrumentalities before their minds, while they were providing against its being used as an instrument of tyranny by carefully restricting the penalty, when they knew it had been used as a means of political oppression—can any believe that it was their intention, or, more, properly, that it is the true intent of the Constitution, when it does not so declare, that impeachments may be resorted to by the successful political party to disable the party defeated from rallying for another contest; that it was intended to place in the Constitution an instrumentality by means of which a popular leader, who perhaps alone could rally the party out of power, could be destroyed; that it is the intent of the Constitution that when the archives have passed into the custody of political opponents, papers misplaced, lost, or intentionally suppressed, that then one who had been honored by the people, had laid down his office without any charge against him—that then he should be called upon, away from his district, without jury, no matter what the lapse of time, to answer a charge the penalty of which is perpetual infamy? My regard for the interests of this nation's future, as well as my sense of justice, were I at liberty, in the absence of any such provision, to have any judgment on the subject, would revolt at any such conclusion.

But it may be said that if an officer cannot be impeached after he is out of office the guilty officer will defeat the provision of the Constitution by resigning when he finds he is about to be impeached; that he may then be elected again; and so a vicious officer hold place.

I answer that if he resigns, removal, the main object of impeachment, is effected.

He is not likely to be elected again; the interests of the nation are safe with the people and with that public sentiment which they create. But, besides, a remedy for this objection can readily be provided by statute by adding the penalty of disqualification to hold office on any one who shall be convicted of crime while in or which relates to any civil office. We have now such a penalty on our statutes as to some crimes.

The provisions of the Constitution on this subject are very few and plain, and may be thus stated :

The Constitution provides—

First. Who may impeach; namely, the House only.

Second. Who may try ; namely, the Senate only.

Third. For what impeachment may be presented ; namely, for treason, bribery, or other high crimes and misdemeanors.

Fourth. What shall be the judgment; namely, removal from office or removal from office and disqualification.

Fifth. Who may be impeached ; namely, the President, Vice President, and all civil officers of the United States.

In the light of these express provisions it is strange that any one should claim that the provision that "the House of Representatives shall have the *sole* power of " impeachment " has the effect of importing the entire English system of impeachment, and that consequently one need not be in office to be subject to the proceeding.

We have been referred to a few authorities on this subject. Rawle, in his work on the Constitution, says, " It is obvious that impeachment extends only to those " in office or to those who have been ; " and this is claimed to be an authority in favor of the right to impeach one who has ceased to be an officer. I do not so understand it. Mr. Rawle directly negatives the idea that the impeachment procedure of Great Britain has any place in our Constitution, by saying it is restricted to those who are or who have been *in office.* Again, he is stating a limitation, and says in the *alternate* that it is obvious that the power of impeachment extends "only to those in office or to those who have been." That, few will question.

The Blount case has been referred to. It is this: It appears that Blount was a Senator and had been expelled. His counsel pleaded : 1. That senatorship was not an office. 2. That he was no longer a Senator. It was decided that the Senate had not jurisdiction. Will any one claim that, if the common parliamentary law of England had been introduced into our Constitution by its provision that " the House of Representatives shall have the sole power of impeachment," the Senate would not have had jurisdiction over Mr. Blount's case? It would unquestionably have had jurisdiction.

Barnard's case has been referred to. He was in a civil office when impeached ; the judgment of removal was the very judgment that was needed ; and the fact that his offense was committed during a prior term separated from its then existing term only by an imaginary point of time does not affect the question. There is no provision of the Constitution that I know of that would prevent a civil officer from being impeached while in office for a crime committed before he became such officer.

Kent, in his Commentaries, (volume 1, pages 288 and 289,) treats impeachment simply as a procedure for the removal of civil officers who have been guilty of crime.

The convention that formed the present constitution of New Jersey had submitted to it by its committee provisions relative to impeachment identical with those of the Constitution of the United States. On motion of Chief Justice Hornblower, that convention, composed of distinguished jurists, extended the liability of civil officers for two years after the expiration of their term, thereby showing that in their opinion the liability to impeachment under the Federal Constitution was only while in office.

Nearly ninety years have passed since the adoption of our Constitution, and it does not appear that the procedure by impeachment has in any State in the Union or under the Federal Government been invoked against any one who was not in office.

Proceedings in impeachment in the States and under the General Government have been commenced and have uniformly been discontinued on the resignation of the accused.

Justice Story, in his Commentaries on the Constitution, gives the most thorough dissertation on the subject of impeachment that is anywhere to be found. There is scarcely an authority that he does not refer to or a view that he does not consider. The question we have before us not having been adjudicated, he expresses himself with his usual deference ; but no one can read the eight hundred and first section of the second volume of his Commentaries and doubt that the great jurist was clearly of opinion that one could not be impeached except while in office. He says :

"As it is declared in one clause of the Cons'itution that 'Judgment in cases of im-
"peachment shall not extend further than to removal fr m office and disqualification
"to hold and enjoy any office of honor, tr ist or profit under the United States,' and in
"another clause that 'the Pr-sident. Vice P esident and all civil officers of the United
"States, shall be removed from office on impe chment for, and conviction of treason,
"bribery, or other high crimes and misdemeanors,' it would seem to follow that the
"Senate were bound on the conviction in all cases to enter a judgment of removal
"from office, though it has a discretion as to inflicting the punishment of disqualifica-
"tion. If, then, there must be a judgment of removal from office it would seem to
"follow that the Constitution contemplated that the party was still in office, at the
"time of the impeachment. If he was not, his offense was still liable to be tried and
"punished in the ordinary courts of justice.
"And it might be argued with some force that it would be a vain exercise of author-
"ity to try a delinquent for an impeachable offense when the most important object for
"which the remedy was given was no longer necessary or attainable. And although a
"judgment of disqualification might still be pronounced, the language of the Constitu-
"tion may create some doubt whether it can be pronounced without being coupled
"with a removal from office. There is also much force in the remark that an impeach-
"ment is a proceeding purely of a political nature. It is not so much designed to
"punish an offender as to secure the state against gross official misdemeanors. It
"tou hes neither his person nor his property, but simply divests him of his political
"capacity."

My opinion is that the Senate has no jurisdiction to try William W. Belknap.

SERVICE OF WRITS OF MANDAMUS.

Mr. FRELINGHUYSEN said :

Mr. President, I wish to say a few words in reference to the bill as it now stands. When a law is to be passed, the proper inquiry is, what is the evil that is sought to be remedied? The evil is simply this: Municipal corporations in a number of States of the Union, such as cities, townships, counties, have by their Legislatures, been authorized to issue bonds for the building of railroads and for other purposes. The same law which authorized the issue of the bonds provided that the municipality should be taxed at a given rate, 1 per cent. or a ½ per cent., as the fact might be, a sum sufficient to pay the interest on those bonds. On the credit of those bonds, railroads have been constructed. The inhabitants of the municipality have the convenience resulting from them and their property has been appreciated by those railroads. For one or two years, the coupons are paid ; then the default is made in the payment of the coupons. Suits are instituted in the Federal courts and judgments obtained. The next process is to issue an execution, which, of course, is returned "No goods," and the next process is a mandamus from the court directing the proper officers of the county or other municipality to proceed to execute the State law and to raise the sum which the State has directed should be raised. The penalty, if the officer does not perform this duty, is punishment for contempt of the mandate of the court. To avoid this punishment and to avoid raising the money, these officers resign, and that as the law stands is an end of the power of the court. This act authorizes the court, in the event of such resignation, to appoint other persons to carry out the directions of the State and enforce the law and the judgment.

These bonds are held by individuals all over the United States. I saw a statement that in the State of Maine alone the savings banks of that State have a million dollars of them. They are held by persons of limited means in New Jersey.

Now, any person who thinks that a subordinate State officer by his wrongful act should defeat the judgment of the courts of the United States ought not to vote for this bill; but that any person who thinks that a subordinate State officer should not have that power should vote for this bill.

That a mandamus is the proper remedy in such case, I read from the second volume of Dillon on Municipal Corporations, section 687 :

" Where the law under which the debt was incurred provides for the levy of a special " tax to pay it, this duty will be enforced by mandamus, and in such a case it is no " answer to an application for this remedy that an execution has not been returned " *nulla bona* or that the corporation debtor may have property subject to a sale on exe- " cution."

The Federal courts, as the law now stands, have no power to enforce these judgments. They can only act through the officers appointed by the State. That has been settled in two cases: first, in the case of the Board of Levy in the State of Louisiana for the parishes of Carroll and Madison, which issued bonds. They would not levy the tax, although authorized by the State to do it. The creditors sought in that case by a bill in equity to enforce a contribution from the inhabitants, but the court said that that remedy would not answer, the only remedy was a mandamus, and the only manner in which a mandamus can be enforced is according to law.

That Congress has full power to pass this act, and that it is a duty incumbent upon it, there can be no question. The Constitution of the United States provides that—

" The judicial power of the United States shall be vested in one Supreme Court, and " in such inferior courts as the Congress may from time to time ordain and establish."

The Federal courts have no judicial power excepting as the Federal Legislature gives it to them, and we omit to perform a clear duty under the Constitution by refusing to pass such a law.

Story says, in his second volume, page 445 :

" To suppose that it is not an obligation on Congress to vest this power in the Federal " courts, but that it might omit or decline to do it is to suppose that, under the Consti- " tution, Congress might defeat the Constitution itself."

That is in reference to the creation of inferior courts. And again, on page 435, he says :

" The judiciary must be so organized as to carry into complete effect all the purposes " of its establishment. It must at once possess the power and means to check usurpa- " tion and enforce the execution of its judgments."

The Constitution declares that Congress may create inferior tribunals and then provides that it shall have power to pass all laws to carry into effect the foregoing provision. In the case of the Supervisors *vs.* Rogers, which is reported in 7 Wallace, page 180, this question came before the Court. The State of Iowa, for the enforcement of its State judgments, had passed such a law as we are now considering, providing that where the officers resigned, the courts should have power to appoint other persons to perform their duties. By the laws of the United States the Federal courts have the right to adopt the procedure of the State courts ; and in that case, where the officers who had to levy and collect the tax resigned, the circuit court of the United States, following that State act, did appoint others to perform the duty, and the collection was made.

Not to pass this act seems to me to be the greatest injustice ; it is to permit the Federal courts of the nation to be treated with contempt ; it is the authorization on the part of Congress of repudiation. If the judgments of a State court are not enforced, the fault is with the State Legislature ; if the judgments of the national courts are not enforced, the fault is with the national Legislature. It is not the province of the State courts to see that the judgments of the Federal courts are enforced. If, as in the case of Iowa, the States wish to avoid the evil we are considering as to their State courts, they can pass such a law, and under such legislation the national court can come in and take advantage of the State procedure, but when in any State, as in New Jersey or in New York, there is no such necessity, there being no such resignations by the officers, it then becomes incumbent on us to supply that defect of legislation.

Besides, Mr. President, this law would be of more advantage to the townships, counties, and cities that it is intended to reach than any law that can be passed. It will be a benefit to the debtor as well as to the creditor. The most important and valuable right that a State has is the right and power to make a contract; and nothing is a contract that cannot be enforced in despite of the will of the party who makes it. That is the very essence of a contract. The Constitution has guarded that great right by saying that the State shall not pass any law impairing the obligation of a contract. Now let this law be passed, and the result is that only such tax can be collected as is in accordance with State legislation, and such will be collected. The people of the country will see that there is power in the Federal courts to enforce their judgments, and consequently that the bonds of these cities will be paid and are good, and these bonds, which are now bearing 8 and 10 per cent., can be refunded at 5 or 6 per cent., at a great saving to the municipality. It is clearly for the benefit of the debtors as well as of the creditors.

I trust, Mr. President, that this act will receive the approbation of the Senate.

THE MISSISSIPPI ELECTION.

The Senate resumed the consideration of the resolution submitted by Mr. MORTON December 15, 1875, as modified by him on the 27th instant—

Mr. FRELINGHUYSEN said:

Mr. President, I had occasion yesterday to say that under the first clause of the fourteenth amendment, which declares that every one born in the United States shall be a citizen thereof, taken in connection with the last clause of that amendment, which gives Congress the power by legislation to enforce the foregoing, a citizen of the United States had the right of being protected in the exercise of suffrage where it had been conferred upon him. To that my friend from North Carolina [Mr. MERRIMON] takes exception, and he tells us that the Supreme Court have decided otherwise. I beg my friend's pardon. The Supreme Court have never touched that question. There have been four cases decided in reference to the three amendments. One was the Slaughter-house case, to which he has referred, where the question was whether the fourteenth amendment did not secure every citizen against business monopolies. It did not relate in any manner to the question of suffrage. The next case was that of Minor vs. Happersett, the case alluded to by the Senator, where a female applied for the license to practice in the Supreme Court of the United States, found in 21 Wallace. That had no reference to the question of suffrage. The next case was the Grant Parish case, which was this: A number assembled at Colfax, in Grant Parish, Louisiana; a mob took away their arms, broke up the meeting, and murdered thirty of the number. This case has recently been decided by the Supreme Court. It involves the construction of the sixth section of the enforcement act, which is directed against conspiracies to deprive citizens of rights granted or secured by the Constitution of the United States. The court does not dispute the constitutionality of the sixth section of that act; but the decision reached is that the indictment did not charge that any one had interfered with rights which, in the opinion of the Court, were granted and secured by the Constitution. That indictment, which I had occasion to look at, contained thirty-two different counts. The rights under the Constitution which it was charged had been violated were the right of peaceably assembling according to the first article of amendments, the right of bearing arms, and other rights named in the ten amendments to the Constitution. The Supreme Court decided within the last week that those amendments, as has been understood by us all, were only inhibitions and restrictions on Congress, and did not confer any rights on citizens.

There was another count in the indictment charging a violation of the fourteenth amendment, in that citizens had been deprived of life and property without due process of law. The court took the view which has been suggested by the Senator from North Carolina, that the fourteenth amendment, when it says that no State shall abridge the privileges and immunities of citizens of the United States, is a prohibition on State legislation and not on individuals. From this view I dissent, as the amendment further provides that the State shall not deny to any person equal protection of the laws. The only case under these amendments which has ever been decided by the Supreme Court in reference to suffrage that I am aware of is the recent case of United States vs. Reese and Foushee. And what was that case? There was an indictment against inspectors of election for refusing the vote of a colored man on account of his race and color. It was refused because he did not present evidence of having paid his tax, which was a prerequisite to voting, but he did present his affidavit to the effect that he had offered to pay his tax, and that the wrongful act of the tax-collector had prevented his tax being paid.

In this case the Court say, in brief, that the first section of the enforcement act is only declaratory, there being no sanction annexed ; that the second section does not apply to inspectors of election, and these defendants were inspectors ; that the third section is a general regulation, and does not make the crime to depend upon depriving one of a vote on account of race, color, or previous condition of servitude—which is an essential quality to a crime under the fifteenth amendment—and that therefore there was no case. If there had been six more words in the act of Congress, to wit, "on account of race or color," the law would have described a crime under a constitutional law.

I do not see that any one can much object to that decision.

Mr. MERRIMON. The Court do not say so. The Court say expressly that Congress has as yet not legislated in such a way as to execute the fifteenth amendment, and what legislation is necessary for that purpose the Court do not undertake to say or suggest.

Mr. FRELINGHUYSEN. I have read that decision. I repeat what I have said. The clear effect of the decision is that the objection to the law is that it is a general regulation, applicable to the rejection of any vote, instead of only making it a crime, as does the amendment, to deprive one of a vote on account of race, color, or previous condition of servitude. The entire reasoning of the Court takes that view. It considers the question whether the first section, with the third and fourth taken together, amounts only to a prohibition against rejecting a vote on account of race and color ; but, being a penal statute, the Court decide that the statute is not capable of being so construed. I think my friend will agree with me that, if there had been six more words in the statute, the Court would have given judgment for the plaintiffs in error. But that is not important to my purpose.

One thing is certain: the question whether Congress has not by legislation the right to protect the citizen, who has been invested with the right to vote, from being deprived of his vote by violence or fraud has never been adjudicated against in this country. The Court say in express words in the only decision they have made relative to voting since the amendments were adopted, that their whole decision rests upon the fifteenth amendment; counsel for the plaintiffs in error having given up all claim that the case was to be sustained under the fourteenth. Whether that was wise is not now the question.

Mr. MERRIMON. Passing by what the Court said—in fact, they said nothing on that subject—I beg my honorable friend to explain to the Senate how he derives the power from the fifteenth amendment that he claims?

Mr. FRELINGHUYSEN. I will. There is, then, we see, nothing in the decisions of the Supreme Court, upon which my friend has placed himself, declaring that suffrage when conferred and as conferred upon a citizen is not a right of a citizen which Congress may by proper legislation under the first and last clauses of the fourteenth amendment protect. Now let us go on a step further. Is the right to vote a natural right?

MR. MERRIMON. No, sir.

Mr. FRELINGHUYSEN. No; we agree. And yet it comes very near to it. Where does the right come from? From the Constitution. How does it get into the Constitution? It is placed there by the convention. Who make the convention? The people. How is their will made known? Only by voting. So, sir, while I agree voting is not a natural right—government could exist without it and could be formed without it—it is the initial step in civilization.

Mr. MERRIMON. Voting is not a civil right.

Mr. FRELINGHUYSEN. It is not a natural right. And now I ask, is voting a necessary incident to citizenship?

Mr. MERRIMON. No, sir.

Mr. FRELINGHUYSEN. No, of course it is not; if it were, every woman and child would have the right to vote. Neither one of these two propositions, however, conflicts with my position, that when by law the right to vote is given to a citizen it is right to be protected from being violently and fraudulently taken from the citizen. Unless the right of citizenship was a mere decoration, it carries with it protection to its incidents, protection in the exercise of that suffrage which the law has conferred. The proposition is too plain to be questioned. My friend will not question that North Carolina has the right to protect its citizen from being deprived by fraud and violence of the right the law has conferred upon him. He will not deny that it is the duty of his State thus to do, and that too because of the citizenship of him who claims the protection. It is the same with a citizen of the United States.

Citizenship of a State confers all the rights that grow out of the constitution and laws of the State. Citizenship of the United States confers all the rights that grow out of the Constitution and laws of the United States. That is clear. Does not the right to vote for Representatives grow out of the Constitution of the United States?

Mr. MERRIMON. It does not.

Mr. FRELINGHUYSEN. I insist that it does, sir.

Mr. MERRIMON. Then we are at issue.

Mr. FRELINGHUYSEN. But for the Constitution of the United States no man would have a right to vote for a Representative. The Constitution of the United States in express terms creates United States voters, United States electors, and specifies their qualifications.

Mr. MERRIMON. It provides that the State may provide them, expressly.

Mr. FRELINGHUYSEN. The Constitution of the United States says:

"The House of Representatives shall be composed of members chosen every second "year by the people of the several States, and the electors in each State shall have "the qualifications requisite for electors of the most numerous branch of the State "Legislature."

This Constitution provides that there shall be United States electors, and specifies as their qualifications that they shall have the same that are required in the State for the most numerous branch of the Legislature. Not only that, but this Constitution further provides, by the fourth section of the fifth article, that Congress shall have the right to regulate the manner in which those United States electors shall cast their votes.

Before the recent amendments to the Constitution I agree that United States citizenship was a very vague thing. One article of the Constitution declared " that "citizens in each State should be entitled to all the privileges and immunities of "citizens of the several States." That only created an equality of right; that only said that there was to be no discrimination. In the Dred Scott case it was established that every State had the right to fix and determine upon the qualification of its own citizens; that it had a perfect right to say that one of African blood

4

should not be a citizen. Such was the condition of the law when the fourteenth amendment was adopted, and that changed all this and established it that every person born or naturalized in the United States and subject to the jurisdiction thereof should be a citizen of the United States and of the State in which he resides. Before that amendment citizenship of the United States, except in the single case of naturalization, was derivative from State citizenship, and the State could exclude one-half or nine-tenths of all her people from being citizens of the United States.

Then we have this case: Before the amendment, there were United States electors with specified qualifications. Before the amendment, Congress had the right to regulate the manner in which those electors should cast their votes. The Constitution has since placed a restriction even on the States as to what qualifications United States electors shall possess, and has said that they shall be exempt from discrimination on account of race or color. We have then under the Constitution United States electors, we have their qualifications fixed, we have modified those qualifications, and the nation has declared in express words that there shall be a United States citizenship, and has declared that Congress shall have all power by appropriate legislation to carry into effect this grand declaration of United States citizenship. This is the sublime rescue of the war. Can it now be denied that, where the citizen has by law the right to vote, Congress has the power to protect this right from fraud and violence? Sir, it is to accuse this nation of an imbecility with which no nation on the earth can be charged. Is it true that this nation alone of all the world, with a written Constitution declaring that there shall be a national citizenship which should give protection in every nook and corner of the world, is unable to afford its citizens any succor? Is it true that the proud cry "I am an American citizen," is to become a shame and a hissing in the earth? No, sir, we have the right and the power too to protect American citizenship at home and abroad.

    *   *   *   *   *   *   *   *   *   *

The Senator complains that we have willfully spent time here in differing from the Supreme Court. The Senator must be a true Calvinist, for he not only thinks that everybody should believe as he believes, but that they should be punished for their unbelief. I do not propose myself to do anything that I know will damage this country much, nor do I propose to be lectured very much as to the manner in which I discharge my duties as Senator.

As to the Supreme Court, let me say that I have as much respect for their decisions as any man in the country; but what is a decision? It is the adjudication of the question before the Court, and their opinion that legitimately grows out of the question, that is entitled to all consideration; but the dicta that may be scattered through their opinions are not law to us.

The question that we were discussing was not, as my friend has said, whether the constitutional amendments gave the right of suffrage. No one has pretended that the Constitution, or any of the amendments, conferred the right of suffrage. Ordinary attention to the debate would have shown the Senator that that was not the position insisted upon. The claim was that where the citizen had by law the right of suffrage the National Government had the power to protect that right from being destroyed by violence and fraud; a very different proposition from that which he has argued. He refers to the decisions of the Supreme Court. What are they? One is the question whether monopolies did not violate the fourteenth amendment. Another, a case to which he refers and in view of which he asks our abject subservience to the Supreme Court, is whether a female can practice law in the United States courts. What have those decisions to do with the question before us? More than that, the Supreme Court have not ever put forth any dictum that I am aware of denying that Congress had the right, where suffrage existed as a right, to protect it from being destroyed by violence or fraud. This is a right that I claim not as the Senator states in behalf of the black man. I claim it, sir, for the white man as well as the colored. I hope to see the day when everywhere in this broad land, South and North, East and West, every citizen will be protected not only in his suffrage, but in his property, his life, and his liberty. Then we will have peace.

JAPANESE INDEMNITY FUND.

The Senate, as in Committee of the Whole, resumed the consideration of the bill (S. No. 6.6) in relation to the Japanese Indemnity fund.

Mr. FRELINGHUYSEN said:

Mr. President, I had not intended to trouble the Senate with any remarks on this subject. Having made a report in favor of the bill, I proposed there to leave the measure ; but finding that there are some Senators, distinguished alike for their regard to the national honor and for their care of the public Treasury, who have doubts in reference to it, and as this is the voluntary payment of a large sum of money, I think it right that I should briefly and plainly state the reasons why the United States should not retain the Japanese indemnity fund.

We all know, sir, that for centuries the Japanese looked upon intercourse with other nations as destructive of their prosperity. They feared that if the Anglo-Saxons gained a foot-hold in their country they would subjugate them, or that they would at all events make their wealth tributary to them ; and it seems to me that for that fear there is some apology in the history of Great Britain in the Oriental world. Intercourse with foreigners is repulsive to their traditions, their tastes, and their pride. Such, without multiplying words, was the state of public sentiment. Now let us look for a minute at the governmental and political condition of that country.

The universally acknowledged sovereign of Japan was the Mikado. He claimed by hereditary succession, commencing prior to the Christian era and continuing for twenty-five centuries. The commander-in-chief of Japan was the Tycoon, who had held his position by succession for about two centuries. He was the executive of the government. Thus there seemed to be a dual government, the Mikado having his court at Kioto, in the northwestern part of Japan, and the Tycoon having his court at Yedo. The Tycoon, partly because he came more in contact with foreigners and partly because he saw personal commercial advantage, entered into treaties with the members of the allied powers—England, France, the Netherlands, and the United States. It seems as if the Tycoon had no right to make these treaties, and as if the treaty which was made with us—and this is worthy of observation—was defective.

Commodore Perry went to Japan in 1853. He used no coercion to effect these treaties. All he did was to take his big ship up in waters where a foreign man-of-war had never before floated, within a mile of Yedo, and there may have exercised a persuasive constraint upon the opinions of that people. In 1854 he made a treaty. It was only a treaty of amity. In 1858 a treaty of commerce was effected. These defective treaties were ratified by the Mikado in 1866, after the contest to which our attention will be called had occurred. This you will see by referring to the diplomatic correspondence of 1866-'67, pages 191, 192, and 193. There Mr. Portman, who was our consul and the successor of Mr. Pruyn, in 1865, made this report to Mr. Seward :

"The treaties, as well as all the acts of the Tycoon's government in pursuance thereof, "have now become legalized, and the Tycoon is said to be again the supreme executive "authority in this empire. It is deemed quite probable that the Choshu rebellion will "now be satisfactorily disposed of without resort to coercive measures."

Again he says :

"I believe I am not too sanguine when venturing to submit it, as my opinion, that "the formal sanction of the treaties by the Mikado, recognized by all Japanese as the "real sovereign of their country, will prove an important result of the recent negotia-"tions, due, in a great measure, no doubt, to the perfect unanimity of views and action "of the foreign representatives."

And Mr. Portman, in a letter to the Tycoon, November 21, 1865, says :

"By approving the obligations entered into by your majesty with foreign powers, the "Mikado and the daimios will make an end to existing difficulties and avert future "dangers."

And on the 6th of December, 1865, Mr. Portman, writes to Mr. Seward.

"I have the honor to transmit herewith (No. 1) translation of a letter from the minis-
"ter for foreign affairs, announcing that the Mikado's ratification of the treaties was
"promulgated in all parts of this empire on the 1st instant."

Thus we see, Mr. President, that at the time this controversy took place between
Japan and this country there was at best a defective treaty, one which we were
very happy subsequently to have ratified by the Mikado, the true sovereign of
Japan.

In 1862 and 1863 the daimios, who were influential princes, one of them at least,
Choshu, the daimio of Sugato, perhaps as powerful as the Mikado himself, determined to oppose this intercourse with foreigners. They did this because of their
traditional antipathy to foreigners; their motto being that " that country is wisely
" governed which never changes its organic law." They were also opposed to the
treaties, because they thought, and probably correctly, that the Tycoon had usurped
authority in inaugurating these great fundamental changes in their country by
means of treaties which he had no lawful authority to make.

The opposition of the daimios compelled the Tycoon to temporize. He was
obliged to appear at times to them, and probably to the Mikado, to be in favor of
the expulsion of foreigners, and he was obliged to act as their executive, while, at
the same time, it is true that he faithfully fulfilled all the provisions of the treaties,
as subsequent events have proven. That this was the position of the Tycoon
appears by the Diplomatic Correspondence of 1864-'65, pages 468, 529, and 530,
which is as follows:

" *Mr. Pruyn to Gorogio, Minister of the Tycoon, December,* 1863.

" It is impossible to avoid the conclusion that the government of His Majesty the
"Tycoon urged my withdrawal from Yedo because it was aware of the existence of a
"party hostile to my residing there, and because it was apprehensive for my safety. It
"is also evident that the government, instead of insisting that the subjects of His Maj-
"esty the Tycoon should submit to the treaties, desired to conciliate the hostile daimios
"by rendering the treaties practically void so far as they guarantee a safe residence in
"that city. It was for this reason the suggestion was made that Yedo would be less safe
"during the absence of His Majesty the Tycoon, while, to my mind, directly the reverse
"was the fact. The assemblage of many daimios at Kioto and the withdrawal of so
"many of their retainers from Yedo appeared to me to constitute a great element of
"safety.

" *Memorandum of Conversation between the Representatives of Allies in* 1874.

"The Tycoon, by treating with foreigners on a footing of equality, has hurt the
"national pride of the daimios, while he damaged their interests by reserving to him-
"self the monopoly of our new commercial relations.

"To these causes of the discontent of the daimios have soon been added the increase
"of taxes and other exactions imposed on them under the pretext of providing for the
"defense of the country.

"This hostile attitude has been the more clearly defined from the Tycoonship having
"just passed into weak hands, and the best guarantee of its power was given up when
"the daimios, whom it was the custom to keep in Yedo as hostages, were allowed to
"retire to their territories These elements of opposition have naturally been concen-
"trated round the Mikado, who can, at his pleasure, resume the exercise of power
"which his ancestors and himself had simply delegated.

"The members of the high aristocracy could not allow this occasion to pass without tak-
"ing revenge for the long domination of a dynasty, the founder of which had not even
"been their equal in rank; and they have put aside their respective rivalries in order
"to combine and more effectually to attack the reigning Tycoon on the foreign ques-
"tion as his weak point."

And the dispatch of Sir Rutherford Alcock to Earl Russell, of August 25, 1864,
(page 86 of the British State Papers of 1865.) That dispatch is as follows:

" A fixed resolve to effect the expulsion of foreigners from Yokohama, and a stoppage
"of their trade, by the old system pursued with the Dutch, prevails at the court of the
"Mikado. A powerful confederation of daimios exists for the declared purpose of sup-
"porting and carrying out this policy with all the means at their command, and the
"Tycoon with his tributary daimios and adherents are menaced in their existence if
"they do not adopt it. The Tycoon's life and his power are virtual sovereign are both
"plotted against. And latterly pressed between two irreconcilable parties, each wielding
"superior forces to his own, the faction of daimios, acting in the name of the Mikado,
"the titular and only acknowledged sovereign of the empire, and foreign powers claim-
"ing the execution of treaties, the Tycoon and his councilors alike seem to have been

"distracted by contending fears, and bewildered with divergencies of opinion as to the
" course to be followed. The expulsion of foreigners or the maintenance of treaties, pre-
" sented as the sole alternatives, each bringing their own danger, has been a cause of
" violent di-sensions in the palace at Yedo, and ended with the sudden dissolution of
" the cabinet. The concentration of ships and troops here having latterly left no doubt
" that there were foreign powers determined to maintain their treaty rights, and one,
" at least, both able and willing to resist by force of arms if necessary any overt attempt
" to drive them and their trade from this port, has no doubt had much to do with this
" political crisis.
" The Tycoon and his council, pressed by reiterated commands from Kioto to expel
" the foreigners, and convinced as they are now that the resolute attitude taken by my-
" self and colleagues, and the material means collected for resistance, meant war f any
" act of hostility were committed either by the Japanese government or daimios, have
" no doubt been sore perplexed as to what course might best be s cered under such per-
" ilous conditions with a Scylla and Charytdis visible on either hand."

The letter of the daimio of Nugato, Choshu, to the allied representatives is thus
accounted for. He speaks of the Tycoon as being opposed to the treaty powers, as
follows, (Diplomatic Correspondence, 1864 and 1865, page 578:)

" Having fired upon foreign ships in the Straits of Simonoseki last year, in obedience
" to the order of the Mikado and Tycoon, I cannot understand why I was censured by
" tne Tycoon's government as having done wrong in firing. This made it appear as if
" I had disobeyed the orders of the Mikado; and my two retainers having returned a
" short time ago with communications, from the foreign ministers, I became desirous
" to refer again to the Mikado in order to obtain his decision. Nagato-no kami, (son
" and heir to the Prince of Choshu,) set out for Kioto, but before he had arrived dis-
" turbances arose in the capital which, I regret very much to say, obliged hi o to return
" without having accomplished the end in view. I have sent Matsu Shimakoso and Ito
" Shunske to explain to you, and I hope you will understand that henceforth I will
" offer no opposition to the free passage of the Straits of Simonoseki.
                    "SOVEREIGN PRINCE OF SUWO AND NAGOTO IN JAPAN.
" Eighth month, third day, of the first year of Genji, (3d September, 1864.")

It is clear that that was only the apology of a defeated rebel, for he knew that
the Tycoon acted by compulsion as the executive, as appears also from Adams'
History of Japan, pages 305, 306, and 353 ; as follows :

" In words the Tycoon's envoys have assured my colleagues of France and myself
" that the Mikado's edict of expulsion, conveyed to the representatives of the treaty
" powers as a matter f obligation by the Tycoon, was a dead letter with respect to all
" action in regard to it.
" It was no doubt at that period, especially owing to the isolation in which foreigners
" lived, most difficult to ascertain the true state of affairs and to reconcile seeming
" contradictions, but I think it is quite clear now that the Shōgun's ministers were sin-
" cere when they said that the Mikado's edict of expulsion, though conveyed to the
" representatives as a matter of obligation, would in fact be nothing but a dead letter.
        *   *   *   *   *   *   *
" The memorial failed in its object, and the advisers of the Emperor were successful
" in causing His Majesty to turn a deaf ear to all supplications in favor of what must
" now be called the rebellious clan of Chōshin.
" Thus ended 1863, and it seemed that wi er counsels were prevailing at Kiō'o in re-
" gard to the policy toward foreigners, and that from this time, as the native writer
" complains, 'the scheme of expelling the barbarians fell to pieces like ice during a
" thaw.' "

Thus we have this condition of things : a defective treaty ; the daimios opposed
to the government, opposed to the alleged usurpation of the Tycoon, and the
Tycoon obliged to temporize.
Such being the political situation, let us look at the question more directly before
us.
The hostility to the foreigners led to outrages which were committed by the
daimios, as appears by the Diplomatic Correspondence of 1864-'65, volume 3, page
559.

" The governments with which your majesty has made treaties regard those treaties
" as clothed with every sanction necessary to their validity and force. Nor can your
" majesty, without a sacrifice of honor and sovereignty allow any of your subjects to
" deny your perfect right to make such treaties. Your majesty will therefore under-
" stand what I say as neith r intimating nor admitting that any public act is necessary
" to confer rights on the treaty powers not already acquired.
" Their representatives cannot, however, shut their eyes to the fact that several tur-
" bulent and hostile daimios, in order to promote their own selfish purpo es. have en-
" deavored to bring into collision the authority of your majesty and the Mikado to in-
" terrupt your cordial relations, and to render antagonistic powers which, for more than
" two centuries, have been exercised in entire harmony.

" They have. unfortunately, been successful in making the Mikado believe that the
" treaties were injurious to Japan and that they could be annulled. This he has called
" on your majesty to do, leaving no option between opposition to his wishes and a vio-
" lation of he treaties which would eventuate in war.

' Not, therefore. for the purpose of acquiring any rights or privileges for themselves,
" but for the preservation of the ancient polity and laws of Japan and the continuan e
" of the ex rcise of powers by your majesty and the Mikado which have been so long
" in harmonious action the treaty powers, through their repres ntatives, would urge
" the immediate necessity of inducing the Mikado to give th se treaties h s high sanc-
" tion and thus remove every cause of opposition and existing inaucements for hostile
" combinations.

" Your majesty has endeavored to reconcile the obligations thus imposed by the Mi-
" kado with those assumed with the treaty pow rs. Their representatives apprecia-
" ting the difficulties of your position have b en disposed to xercl e great moderation
" and forbearance. But your majesty must now be satl fied that the ime has arrived
" when it is n cessary for you to declare that the treaties must and shall be faithfully
" observed and to abandon all half-way measures."

Among these outrages, they burned down the British legation ; they burned the
American legation at Yedo. On the 16th of June, 1863, the American steamer
Pembroke, a merchantman, passing through the Straits of Simonoseki, was fired upon
from the rebel batteries. This was done by the rebels in defiance of the government of Japan. The topmast of that ship was carried away, and she was otherwise
injured. This insult to our flag the Wyoming properly punished. It is worthy
of remark that the Wyoming contended against a vastly superior force. The
daimios had erected their batteries seventy feet above the level of the sea ; they
had purchased war vessels and had them there, to wit : the brig Alert, clipper-built,
twelve guns, a fast sailer, costing some $45,000 ; the iron British steamer Lance-
field, which cost $160,000 ; the American bark Webster, which cost $22,000 ; and
the American bark Lanrick. It is important to observe the character of the force
with which the Wyoming contended, because the amount of prize-money, if any,
that she would under certain circumstances have been entitled to under our law
depends in a degree on that fact.

The Wyoming on the 26th of June, 1863, ran close along the batteries and
shelled them. Men were seen to jump from the heights into the sea. She made
her course between the two vessels which were there, the Lanrick and the Lancefield. She sent a ball through the stern of the Lanrick and sank her. She sent
another ball through the boiler of the Lancefield, and produced an explosion by
which, according to the report, some forty men were killed. Mr. George S.
Fisher, our consul at Yokohama, says the vessels and property destroyed, besides
the loss of life, were worth $350,000. All this appears by the following dispatch
of Mr. Pruyn to Mr. Seward, in the second volume of the correspondence of 1863
and 1864, pages 1132 and 1133 :

" My anxiety was relieved by the return of the Wyoming early in the morning of the
" 20th instant.

" From a copy of the report to the Secretary of the Navy, with which I have been
" furnished by Commander McDougal, it appears he entered the straits, on the 16th in-
" stant, from the eastward, passing up the Bungo Channel. When the Wyoming was
" seen approaching, a signal gun was fired from the first battery. As she rounded the
" point the steamer Lancefield of four guns, the brig Lanrick. of ten guns, and a bark,
" of four guns, were seen anchored opposite the vill ge of Simonoseki All six of the
" batteries fired on the Wyoming as she steamed past them, carrying the national flag
" aft r the first battery had fired—the Wyoming rese ving fire till she reached the ships.

" By skillfully avoiding the main channel on which the guns of he batteries were
" trained, and keeping close to the batteries, the shot and shell mostly passed over the
" vessel, only damaging the rigging. Approaching the vessels against the remon-
" strances of the Japanese pilot, who declared he would run aground, Captain McDougal
" carried the Wyoming between the bark and brig on the one side and the steamer on
" the other, receiving from and delivering broadsides into each of the ships. It was at
" this point the Wyoming was most under fire. Putting the ship about he sent three
" eleven-inch shells into the Lancefield, the last of which exploded her boilers, and she
" was then run aground. The brig Lanrick was sinking as the Wyoml g left, and the
" bark badly injured. The Wyoming then returned through the strait , pouring shot
" and shell into the batteries The steamer Lancefield had the Jap nese flag at the
" peak, but quickly lowered it. The other vessels carried both the flag of Japan and
" that of the prince.

" I regret to have to say that this success was attended with the loss of four seamen
" killed and seven wounded one of whom has since died.

" The loss would have been much more severe had it not been for the skill and judg-
" ment shown by Captain McDougal in avoiding the usual route by the main channel.

"The guns on the batteries were depressed so as to strike the hull of passing ships at
"that point and stakes were set up near the guns giving the range, so that each gun
"could be fired as the foremast of the ship came in range with the stake at the gun.

"The Lancefield was a fine iron steamer of nearly six hundred tons purchased of the
"English firm of Jardine, Mattheson & Co. for the sum of $115,000; and he brig Lanrick,
"formerly in the opium trade pierced for eighteen guns, though carrying only sixteen,
"was purchased of the same firm for $20,000. The bark was built by the Prince of Thi-
"zen and sold by him to the Prince of Nagato.

"The officers of th · custom-house were overheard (as I am informed by the consul-
"general of the Netherlan s, by one of his employés to say that when the boiler of the
"Lancefield exploded forty men were killed, being scalded or suffocated."

This was a gallant achievement of the Wyoming. The resident minister writes
to Mr. Seward that the naval officers looked on and feared the result, and pronounced it a bold and daring deed. It is here worthy of remark as to the passage
of the Straits of Simonoseki that by usage merchantmen had the right to the passage of those waters, but no man-of-war had the right, as I shall show, to pass those
straits. The Pembroke being a merchantman and being fired upon, the Wyoming
was justified in punishing the wrong.

Was not that act of firing on the Pembroke sufficiently punished? Two vessels
were destroyed, with the property on board, worth, as Consul Fisher tells us,
$350,000, and forty men were killed. Was not our flag vindicated? Was not
the account squared? There is a point when the infliction of punishment becomes
tyranny and the exaction of compensation robbery. Not only did we thus vindi-
cate that wrong, but, independent of and prior to the treaty of 1864, Japan paid
us full pecuniary compensation for all the damage that was done the Pembroke,
for the destruction of the American legation at Yedo, and for all demands whatever. They paid all that the United States demanded. We had no possible claim
against Japan at that time. To prove this I will read from the diplomatic correspondence of 1864-'65, page 536. It is a communication from our minister resident, Robert H. Pruyn, to Mr. Seward.

"The indemnity demanded for the legation "—

That is, the burning of the legation at Yedo—

"has been paid; and, notwithstanding former declarations that it would be a disgrace
"to admit it. It was declared to be a just claim, and conceded at once without hesita-
"tion or delay.
"The government placed in my hand, a letter drawn by myself in which they said
"that they had directed the governor of Kanagawa, on the 5th of September, to pay me
"the sum of $1,200 "—

It ought to be $12,000—

"principal and interest of the Pembroke claim. and in which they stated that if not
"paid on that day on the production of my letter it would be receivable for all public
"dues to said amount."

And on page 541, in a letter of Mr. Pruyn to Captain Cicero Price of the
Jamestown, he says:

"The Japanese government having arranged to my satisfaction the claims which I
"had been instructed by the President of the United States to make upon it it is my
"pleasant duty to acknowledge the great assistance which you so promptly rendered
"me in bringing the negotiations to a successful termination."

That letter is dated in August, 1863. This attack by the foreign ships of the
allied powers on Japan was in September, 1864, and at that time we had destroyed
vessels and property to the amount of $350,000, killed forty men, had been paid
every farthing we demanded for the damage to the Pembroke, for the burning of
the legation, and every other possible claim the United States made. Was not
the flag vindicated? Was not the account squarred? Did they owe us one farthing? In September, 1864, the United States, having no demand, joined with the
allied powers in the attack on the batteries in a sea where a ship of war had no
right to float. The rebel batteries were still on the heights of the Straits of
Simonoseki. On the 15th of August, 1864, the representatives of the allied powers
instructed the naval officers to attack those batteries, and, if the batteries did not
fire upon them, notwithstanding to make the attack and to destroy them. This is
seen in the British dispatch, page 80, signed by our minister.

"The undersigned, representatives of treaty powers, having met and taken into con-
"sideration the copy of a minute showing the result of the deliberations of the com-
"manding officers of the respective naval forces assembled at Yokohama, and signed
"on the 1.th instant, have agreed as follows:

"1. To inform the commanding officers aforesaid that they are entirely relieved from
"all responsibility with regard to the defense and security of the settlement

"2. To request them in conformity with the programme of the policy set forth in the
"memorandum of the undersigned dated the 22d of July last, to proceed with all con-
"ve ient speed to open the Straits of Simonoseki, destroying and disarming the bat-
"teries of the Prince of Choshu, and otherwise crippling him in all his means of attack;
"to inform them that the political situation renders it desirable that there should be
"no consid rable delay in the commencement of operations.

"3. In the possibility of the Prince of Choshu being intimidated by the imposing
"nature of the force brought against him, and not firing to request the naval officers,
"notwithstanding, to destroy the batteries and take such means as may be deemed
"practicable to secure a material guarantee against any future hostilities from the same
"quarter.

"4. To request them to avoid entering into any negotiations with the prince, reserv-
"ing the solution of all ulterior questions to the action of the Tycoon's government in
"connection with the foreign representatives.

"5. To suggest that any demonstration of f rce in the vicinity of Osaka be avoided,
"as possibly giving ri-e to -ome new complications, and in order not to change the
"character of this expedition, which ought to be regarded no otnerwise than as a chas-
"tisement to be inflicted on an outlaw or a pirate.

"6 To reque-t the commanding officers to secure the return to Yokohama of such
"part of the squadron as may not be required for the maintenance of a free passage as
"soon as the operations here contemplated shall have been completed.
"Signed this 15th day of August, 1864, at Yokohama.
"RUTHERFORD ALCOCK,
"*Her Britannic Majesty's Envoy Extraordinary,*
"*and Minister Plenipotentiary in Japan.*
"LÉON ROCHER,
"*Ministre Plénipotentiaire de sa Majesté Impériale au Japon.*
"ROBERT H. PRUYN,
"*Minister Resident of the United States in Japan.*
"D. DEGRAEFF VAN POLSBROCK,
"*Consul General and Political Agent of His Netherlands Majesty in Japan.*"

The Japanese government, struggling with a rebellion almost too powerful for
them, struggling because they had made a treaty with us, begged for a little time.
They gave us a reason why they wanted a few days' delay before that attack was
made in their waters by these ships of war, that a rebellion had broken out north
of Yedo. This is found in the British Diplomatic Correspondence, page 81, and
is as follows:

"Taehibana Idzumi no Kami replied that the Gorogio, while acknowledging the ne-
"cessity of proceedings being taken against the Prince of Choshu and the just cause the
"treaty powers had for action, were yet most anxious that no steps should be taken
"at present by any foreign powers. Various causes had tended to interfere with and de-
"lay the adoption of measures to that end by the Tycoon; among others, the breaking
"out of disturbances in the provinces north of Yedo, rendering necessa y the dispatch
"of large bodies of troops in that direction; but it was still the intention of the Ty-
"coon's government to take measures for the removal of the existing obstructions to
"the navigation of the straits.—*British State Papers,* page 81."

It should have been granted then. Earl Russell was of the same opinion, for
his dispatch dated July 26, 1864, was on its way when this attack was made. I
will read that dispatch. It is found in the British Diplomatic Correspondence, page
45. It is to the minister of Great Britain, Sir Rutherford Alcock:

"FOREIGN OFFICE, *July* 26, 1864.
"SIR: I have to state to you with reference to the dispatches which I have lately re-
"ceived from you that H-r Majesty's go ernment positively enjoin you not to under-
"take any military operations whatever in the interior of Japan; and they would in-
"deed regret the adoption of any measures of hostility against the Japan-se govern-
"ment or princes, even though limited to naval operations, unless absolutely required
"by self-defense. The action of the naval an l m litary forces of Her Majesty in Jap n
"should be limited to the defense and protection of Her Majesty's subjects resident
"in Japan and of their property and to the maint nance of our tr aty rights.

"It may be hoped that the power vested in you by Her Maje ty's ord r in council of
"the 7th of January last, to prohibit, or regulate, or restrict the entrance or passage of
"Britih ships into straits or waters of J pan when such entrance or passage may lead
"to acts of disturbance or acts of violen e or in-y otherwise endanger the m intenance
"of peaceful relations or intercourse between Her Majesty's subjects an l the subjects
"of the Tycoon of Japan, will enable you to prevent the occu rence of the necessity
"for any such measures of hostility to obtain reuress for injuries done to British
",vessels."

And on page 66, on the 18th of August, he, deprecating any such act, says—

"That the Tycoon still professes an intention to chastise the Prince of Naga'o for his "hostile acts and that he is promoting, by the most expeditious means in his power, "the construction of barracks for the regiment of British troops which you have' sum- "moned to Yokohama."

Mr. EDMUNDS. What is the date of that dispatch?

Mr. FRELINGHUYSEN. That is on the 18th of August, 1864. The other was on the 26th of July, 1864.

The United States had no possible grievance and they only joined the expedition to show their approval of it, as will be seen by our Diplomatic Correspondence of 1864-'65, page 545, where Mr. Pruyn, September 3, 1864, the day before the attack was made, thus writes:

"I have also been informed by a vice-minister, attended by Takemeto Kai-no-kami "and other governors, that the Tycoon had taken possession of the Yasikis or palaces "of Choshu in Yedo, and would proceed with great vigor to execute the orders of the "Mikado. At the same time he said he had come down to ask that the fleet should not "be sent against him.
"The fleet had, as he was aware, already left. The expedition is composed of nine "British, four Dutch, three French and one United States steamer, (chartered) the "Takiang. The British admiral said he would be willing to order the Jamestown 'o be "towed to Simonoseki, if desired; but, as she would be entirely useless when there it "would only mortify the officers and might embarrass his movements. At the same "time both he, Admiral James and the captain commanding the Netherlands squad- "ron, as well as my colleagues gave it as their opinion that it was exceedingly desira- "ble that our flag should be represented, and that, though the government of Japan "fully understood the position of the United States, the daimios not in the confidence "of the government might misapprehend it, and that, although the Jamestown would "be necessarily retained at this place, it was possible the impression might be created "thereby that the United States was not in harmony with the other treaty powers. "Under these circumstances Captain Price and myself felt it to be our duty to "charter the Tak'ang an American steamer, nearly new, of over six hundred tons, "and which it is supposed will prove quite service able."

So we did not enter into this alliance and join in the attack because we had any reclamations to make or any injury to avenge.

If vessels of war had the right to pass through the Straits of Simonoseki and if rebels in defiance of the government of Japan planted batteries there, I do not know on what principle it is that the government of Japan could be called upon for pecuniary satisfaction. In our recent war we had batteries on the Mississippi, on the Gulf, at Charleston, and elsewhere. Did that fact create any liability on the part of the United States to give remuneration to any one? It certainly did not. But these batteries were on the territory of Japan and commanded waters that were exclusively her territory. No treaty has ever been made opening the straits or inland seas of Japan to any nation. No port had been opened which could naturally be reached through that strait or by those seas.

Mr. EDMUNDS. The Pembroke was going to Nagasaki from Yokohama through Simonoseki, and Nagasaki was an open port.

Mr. FRELINGHUYSEN. The treaty of 1854 opened a port in the northern part of Japan called Hakodadi, which can be seen in the upper part of Japan, and one other, Simoda, which was ingulfed by an earthquake before this transaction and does not appear upon the map.

Mr. EDMUNDS. It was dropped out of the map.

Mr. FRELINGHUYSEN. The treaty of 1858 opened the port of Kanagawa, which is in the eastern part of Japan, and which you cannot by any possibility reach through the inland seas or through the Straits of Simonoseki. They also opened the port of Nagasaki, which is in the southwestern part of Japan, away below the straits, and in no way connected, or by possibility to be reached through those straits. They also opened the port of Nee-egata, which is in the western part of Japan, three hundred miles away from these seas; so that no one of those ports could by possibility be reached through those straits or through those seas. They opened one other port, which could be reached through those seas, which is the port of Hiogo, at the northerly end of those seas, at the extreme limit of them. But although that port was to be opened by these treaties, by an arrangement it was not actually to be opened until 1868, after this whole transaction. This arrangement appears by the following stipulation by our minister, found in Diplomatic Correspondence of 1864–'65, page 484:

"LEGATION OF THE UNITED STATES IN JAPAN,
" KANAGAWA, *January* 23. 1864.

" By virtue of the power vested in me by the President of the United States of " America, I Robert H. Pruyn, minister resident of the United S ates in Japan, do " hereby consent that the time for the opening of the cities and ports of Yedo, Osacca, " Illogo and Nee-egata shall be and is hereby extend d for the period of five years, " dating from the 1st of January, 1863.

" ROBERT H PRUYN,
" *Minister Resident of the United States in Japan.*"

So that there was no port opened by treaty which could be reached through the Straits of Simonoseki or the inland seas.

*   *   *   *   *   *   *

Mr. HOWE. If the Senator will allow me, I should like to ask him whether he does or does not understand that there is a public right secured to all nations of passing through those straits.

Mr. FRELINGHUYSEN. I insist that there is no public right for ships of war to enter or to pass through those straits. There is a right of passage for merchantmen, which is a right established by usage. The Pembroke was lawfully going through those straits when she was fired upon. She was a merchantman, and usage gave her that right. Therefore the Wyoming is commendable in vindicating the rights of the United States; but after those rights were fully vindicated by the destruction of $350,000 worth of property and forty men's lives, after they paid just that bill our Government presented, I say that the claim of this country upon Japan was terminated. In support of the answer I have given to the question put to me by my friend from Wisconsin, I refer to 1 Phillimore on International Law, page 210:

" Though the open sea be thus incapable of being subject to the rights of property or " jurisdiction, yet reason, practice, and authority have firmly settled that a different " rule is applicable to certain portions of the sea.

" And first with respect to that portion of the sea which washes the coast of an inde- " pendent state. Various claims have been made and various opinions pronounced at " different epochs of history, as to the extent to which territorial property and juris- " diction may be extended. But the rule of law may be now considered as fairly estab- " lished namely, that this absolute property and jurisdiction do not extend, unless by " the specific provisions of a treaty or an unquestioned usage, beyond a marine league " (being three miles) or the distance of a cannon-shot from the shore at low tide."

And again, on page 212:

" Besides the rights of property and jurisdiction within the limit of cannon-shot " from the shore, there are certain portions of the sea which though they exceed this " verge, may, under special circumstances, be prescribed for. Maritime territorial " rights extend, as a general rule over arms of the sea bays, gulfs, estuaries which are " inclosed but not entirely surrounded by lands belonging to one and the same state."

Kent, in the first volume of his Commentaries, pages 29 and 30, says:

" Considering the great extent of the line of the American coasts, we have a right to " claim, for fiscal and defensive regulations, a liberal extension of maritime jurisdic- " tion; and it would not be unreasonable, as I apprehend, to assume, for domestic pur- " poses connected with our safety and welfare, the control of the waters on our coasts, " though included within lines stretching from quite distant headlands as, for instance, " from Cape Ann to Cape Cod, and from Nantucket to Montauk Point, and from that " point to the Capes of the Delaware, and from the south cape of Florida to the Missis- " sippi."

*   *   *   *   *

I call attention to another authority. I read from Travers Twiss on Peace, page 250:

" If a sea is entirely inclosed by the territory of a nation, and has no other communi- " cation with the ocean than by a channel of wh ch that nation may take possession, " it appears that such a sea is no less capable of being occupied and becoming property " than the land, and it ought to follow the fate of the country that surrounds it. The " Black Sea, while its shores were in the exclusive possession of the Ottoman Porte, " was an instance of a territorial sea of this character. So likewise straits, which " serve as a communication between two seas, and of which the shores on both sides are " the territory of one and the same nation, are capable of being reduced into the pos- " session of that nation. In the same manner a bay of the sea, the shores of which are

"the territory of one and the same nation, and of which the entrance may be effect-
"ively defended against all other nations is capable of being reduced into the posses-
"sion of a nation. 'By this instance,' writes Grotius, 'it seems to appear that the
"' property and dominion of the sea might belong to him who is in possession of the
"' lands on both sides, though it be open above as a gulf, or above and below as a strait,
"' provided it be not so great a part of the sea as, when compared with the lands on both
"' sides, it cannot be supposed to be a portion of them.' "

I suppose there is no question that that is the law. The fact is that the Straits
of Simonoseki are at one point only half a mile wide, and there is not one of the
straits running into those seas anywhere that is six miles wide.

* * * * * * * . *

That being the case Japan has always had the right to control the seas and the
straits, and had the right to exclude ships of war.
When you come to the case of the Pembroke it is entirely different. There
usage had established the right of the merchantmen to pass through those waters,
and, consequently, the Wyoming is to be commended in vindicating that right.
The expedition on the 5th, 6th, 7th, and 8th of September, 1864, made their
attack upon the batteries. The United States had no insult to avenge, no indemnity to claim. Against the entreaty of a friendly power this attack was made.
When this expedition was over, immediately before the treaty of October, 1864,
under which we received in gold $785,000, Japan was under obligation to pay us
for nothing unless she was under obligation to pay us for the expense of the unlawful attack of September, 1864. The expense of that attack to the United States
was about $12,000, not $785,000 in gold, as appears by the Diplomatic Correspondence of 1864 and 1865, pages 540 and 579. Mr. Pruyn, in writing to Mr.
Seward, page 580, states the charter party for the Takiang. The sixth provision
reads thus:

"The said parties of the second part do engage to pay to the said party of the first
"part, for the charter or freight of said Takiang during the voyage aforesaid which
"shall not exceed the term of one month from the date hereof the sum of $9,500, lawful
"gold c in of the United States, in their draft at thirty days' sight on the Secretary of
"the Navy of the United States, or on the Secretary of State of the United States."

And on page 581 our consul makes the bill of items of the additional expense,
English coal, for fuel, $630; Japan coal, &c., making the whole sum, $1,848. So
the whole amount would be $11,348, for which we received $785,000
Now we come to the treaty which was thus exacted. The treaty is found in
volume 14 of the Statutes at Large, page 665, and provides thus:

"The representatives of the United States of America, Great Britain, France, and
"the Netherlands in view of the hostile acts of Mori Daizen prince of Nagato and
"Suwo which were assuming such formidable proportions as to make it difficult for
"the Tycoon faithfully to observe the treaties having been obliged to send their com-
"bined forces to the Straits of Simonoseki in order to destroy the batteries erected by
"that daimio for the destruction of foreign vessels and the stoppage of trade; and the
"government of the Tycoon on whom devolved the duty of chastising this rebellious
"prince, being held responsible for any damage resulting to the interests of treaty
"powers, as well as the expenses occasioned by the expedition, agree, &c."

I should like to know on what principle of natural justice or of international
law it is that a government contending with a rebellion is bound to pay damages
because it did not put down the rebellion. What principle of law is it that places
a nation under greater obligations to another nation for damages than it is to its
own citizens for not preserving the peace? There is no principle to base such a
claim upon. The very basis of the treaty is such that we would not for one instant
recognize. Then the treaty further provides that they are to pay $3,000,000.

"This sum to include all claims of whatever nature for past aggressions on the part
"of Nagato, whether indemnities ransom for Simonoseki, or expenses entailed by the
"operations of the allied squadrons."

All these claims had been paid, with the exception of $11,348 for the charter-
party of the Takiang, for the fuel and the ammunition. Just what our Government asked Japan paid. We had destroyed $350,000 of their property and killed
forty of their men. We had no earthly claim against that government. We

ought not to exact of. a friendly nation a pretended indemnity which we would refuse to any nation under the sun.

* * * * *

Mr. President, our resident minister at Japan, Mr. Pruyn, writes to Mr. Seward on the 29th of October, 1864, that he is not satisfied with this convention. He says in his letter that he would have preferred two million to three million; strange preference if our claim is just. He says that $3,000,000 was claimed by this treaty, which by its very terms is for indemnity, in order that the sum might be an inducement to the Japanese to open to our country other ports, there being a provision in the treaty that if Japan would open other ports they need not pay the $3,000,000. Here is a treaty of indemnity made exorbitant, made more than our minister says it ought to have been made for $785,000 when they did not owe us in any view but $11,348, so that in order to get rid of the exaction Japan would open the ports which they had a perfect right to keep closed. Then he says that the United States is to be paid rather for the moral support than for the material aid that the Taki-ang afforded.

Mr. President, what is the pecuniary price that the United States ask for the moral support which is put forth against the remonstrances of a friendly power for the promotion of our own interests? We should not charge too highly for moral support, when the expedition which is to render it gives it in the very face of the entreaties for a few days' delay from a friendly power.

The following is from Mr. Pruyn's letter to Mr. Seward, Diplomatic Correspondence 1864-'65, pages 581, 582 :

" The British minister and myself, prior to meeting the Japanese commissioners, had " agreed on $2,000,000 as the sum to ' e paid, and would have had no difficul'ty in its divi-" sion among the powers interested. But some difference was suggested as likely to " arise from the con-iderations whether the moral support afforded was not entitled to " weight in such adjustment and I did not feel that it was incumbent on me to inter-" pose any objection to this view, as the moral support afforded by the United States " was considerably in excess of the material support I was enabled to give. I therefore " readily agreed to the reference of this delicate question to the home governments, with " the understanding that a memorandum which I prepared should be signed and " accompany the convention, so as to provide an equitable basis if any should become " desirable or necessary by reason of payment of the indemnity being demanded by " them. I assented the more readily to the proposition of the envoy of His Imperial " Majesty the Emperor of the French to fix the amount at $3,000,000 because I thought " it more likely to lead to the substitution of a port as a material compensation for the " expenses of the expedition.

" Should the Tycoon be averse to the opening of another port and fail to make such " offer in lieu of the payment of indemnities and expenses, the amount agreed on will " not be regarded as unreasonable. But should he make the offer, it will be at the option " of the four powers to accept it in full or in part payment, and in that event a mode-" rate pecuniary fine may be imposed.

" In either case provision will be made for a reasonable indemnity for injuries sus-" tained by the Wyoming and Monitor and for the insult to our flag offered by the attack " on those vessels, as well as on the Pembroke, the owners of which have received from " the Japanese government a sum which covers their loss as estimated by themselves."

There is no possible justification for our retaining this money.

It has been suggested that to return this money would be establishing a bad precedent. Sir, if considering that the insult to our flag had been fully punished, if considering the fact that neither our nation nor our citizens had sustained any damage; if considering the fact that we were dealing with a feeble friendly people, it is right that we should pay back this money ; it is establishing a precedent to do right, and the sooner we establish such a precedent, and the better and more faithfully we follow it, the more it will be for the glory of our country.

But it has been urged that if we pay back this indemnity money and it shall turn out that the claims brought against the Alabama award do not consume it, then we shall be obliged to pay back to Great Britain the residue of that award. If that result should follow, it ought not to deter us from doing right. But, sir, the claims against that award will consume it, and I fear that for many years after it is gone we shall be pressed to pay claims to be made under that award. The treaty of Washington was this : it fixed certain rules and principles, and then left it to the Geneva tribunal either to refer to arbitration specific claims or to pay to the United States an amount in gross. They saw proper to pay us an amount in gross, which was indemnity for the loss of national wealth, that loss being measured by the losses of a certain class of our citizens included within the principles of the treaty. If they added two or three ciphers to the fifteen million that they paid us, they would not have indemnified this country.

But why talk about that? What considerations are there that apply to this case that would apply to Great Britain? Here is a feeble, friendly power just emerging from the darkness of ages. The British lion would roar with laughter at the idea of this country being conscience-stricken for fear we had got the advantage of Great Britain. She is out of her tutelage; her teeth are cut. Has she not gathered to herself the manufacturing interests of the world? Has she not swept our commerce from the seas? Is she not the great moneyed centre, the vortex that swallows up the wealth of the world and makes every nation pay her tribute?

I hope that the United States will always have a national conscience; but I hope it will be a robust and healthy, and not a morbid, sickly, conscience. When we come to that state of mind, we shall indeed be substituting imbecility for integrity.

Mr. President, by the favor of this people we had opened to us their ports. The inland seas and the approaches to them were their territory. No foreign ship of war had a right to enter those waters. Four powerful nations with seventeen ships of war enter their waters and destroy the batteries. In doing that they did, perhaps, no great injury. It was only an infraction of right. They were rebel batteries. The government of Japan did not want them there. But they did not stop with the destruction of rebel batteries. That being done these four powerful nations with their seventeen ships exact a treaty by which Japan has been obliged to pay $3,000,000 in gold for nothing. It is an exaction that can only be justified on the plea that might makes right. Would we have dealt so with England, with France, or with Germany? Would we have submitted to such an exaction from any nation on the earth? Would we have made such a claim of a nation even inferior to us in power, which was cultured and Christianized? We certainly would not.

It may be true, sir, that the leading nations may modify or reject the just and equitable principles of international law when they are dealing with nations of inferior culture and advancement. It may be true, possibly, though I deny it, that in dealing with Japan as she was in 1863 we need not have been so strict as we would be in dealing with a more enlightened nation; but that consideration fails when we come to consider in 1876 whether we shall cover this money into the Treasury or pay it back. Sir, Japan in these last fourteen years has taken position among the nations of the earth. There never has been a nation which in the same period has made such progress. The office of Tycoon has been swept away. The Mikado has asserted his ancient sway, and now rules over his entire empire with an effective central government. Feudalism and the rule of the daimios have been abolished. The Mikado has ratified the treaties, and the prejudice against foreigners disappears. Japan has ceased to be isolated and secluded and has become a part of the community of the world. A nation of fragments is consolidated. A nation of 33,000,000, inhabiting a country a little more than twice the size of New England, extends her hand to us across the Pacific and asks us to be her friend. She has introduced our machinery and our manufactures, our literature, our science, and our arts. She sends her young men to our colleges, where they are the equal in native ability of our own sons. Her representatives are here with us, and nothing deficient in diplomatic propriety or in social culture or courtesy; and the last tidings that come from Japan are that, instead of every sixth successive day being their day of rest, they have adopted the Christian Sabbath, not as a religious day but as a day of rest, and thus by that act adding another proof that that day was made, and was made for man.

Sir, if it were true that enlightened nations were not bound strictly to carry out the principles of international law toward the cannibals of the South Sea Islands, and might even modify them when in 1863 dealing with Japan, still it is not true that in 1876 we can cover that money into the Treasury, for since 1863 Japan has taken her place in the family of nations and can plead her equality as her title to equity.

I do not suppose that there has ever been a subject before Congress which has had so intelligent a support as the measure of paying back this indemnity. We have had petition after petition. In 1873 we had a petition sent to Congress that we should return this money, from many colleges. I will mention a few of them : Williams, Harvard, Vermont College, Yale, California. Bowdoin, Union, Wesleyan University, Burlington (New Jersey) College, University of Michigan, Oberlin (Ohio) College; Northwestern, Illinois ; Hartsville University, Beloit College, Wisconsin ; Hamilton College, New York ; Ripon, Wisconsin ; Carroll, Wisconsin ; Lafayette ; Howard, Alabama ; Roanoke, Virginia ; Saint Joseph, Missouri, and many others.

*   *   *   *   *   *

Mr. President, the cities and counties and States of the Union are all proposing properly to commemorate the centennial of our freedom. Let the Legislature of the nation now, with the approval of the people, perform this act of magnanimity. It will be the commencement of a new era in the intercourse of nations ; and better than arch or pyramid, exposition or pageantry, will such a deed at such a time signalize that day and be memorable in history.

Now I come to the question how much shall we pay back? We received $750,000 in gold, which, when it reached the Secretary of State, amounted to considerably more by reason of exchange. That sum now amounts, under the care of the Secretary of State, who generally makes everything thrive that he has to do with, to $1,200,000 in gold. A part of the increase is by reason of the appreciation of the securities in which the fund has been placed as from to time transferred. I call the attention of my friend from North Carolina [Mr. MERRIMON] to the fact that the difference between the sum we received from Japan with interest at 6 per cent. and the sum actually now in the fund is $351,681. If we paid them back what we received with 6 per cent. simple interest we should still have $351,681. If we paid them 7 per cent. we should have $300,000. If we paid 10 per cent. we should have $160,000. I understand, and I presume correctly, that the money which was paid us was borrowed from England, a part of it at 7 per cent. and the loan sold at 93, and a part of it at 10 per cent.

My own opinion is that, after making just deductions, if there are any just, we should pay them back the whole sum. I can see that there may be a difference of opinion in reference to this. A very considerable part of this money is, as I have stated, from the appreciation of the securities from time to time in which the fund was invested. Much of it is made up by compounding interest, which Mr. Fish has been very careful to do. But I do not think we want any of this money. It did not come to us in the right way.

A word now as to retaining the $125,000 for the officers and crews of the Wyoming and Takiang. This claim of the Wyoming is for punishing the unlawful attack which was made upon the Pembroke, and has no connection with the unlawful expedition of September, 1864. The treaty of 1864 speaks of that transaction as an item of the indemnification. The officers of the Takiang are not responsible for the character of the attack made in September, 1864, because they obeyed the orders of the representative of the country. These vessels, the Lancefield and Lanrick, were piratical vessels. They were making war and cruising against our Government in defiance of and contrary to the will of their government with whom we had a treaty, and that is just what makes a pirate as we have defined in our statutes. On page 1047 of the Revised Statutes, section 5374, it is enacted that any subject of a nation making war at sea or cruising against a vessel of the United States, contrary to a treaty of the United States with such nation, is a pirate and is to be punished as such. It appears by the Revised Statutes, page 834, section 4296, that if these vessels which were sunk had been brought into port and condemned the crew would have entitled to prize-money. It appears that the value of the property destroyed was $350,000.

Then again, by the Revised Statutes, page 909, section 4635, it is provided that for each person on board a ship of war belonging to an enemy on the destruction of the vessel $100 shall be paid if the enemy is of inferior force, and $200 if it is of equal or superior force to the officers and crew of the ship effecting the destruction. The only technical objection to their receiving this bounty is that they do not come within the provision of the statute because these were not ships belonging to an enemy; they belonged to the pirates, to the daimios; the war was made in direct defiance of the government of Japan.

There are abundant precedents for an allowance of this kind.

Captain Oliver Perry and the officers and crew of his squadron for capturing the British vessels on Lake Erie received $255,000, as appears by the Statutes at Large, volume 3, page 130. In a recent case the officers and crew of the United States ship Kearsage, for the destruction of the Alabama, received $190,000. (17 Statutes at Large, page 53.) Captain Bainbridge, his officers and crew, for the destruction of the British frigate Java, received as prize-money $50,000. (2 Statutes at Large, page 818.)

Mr. President, I think that the officers and crews of these vessels should be paid; but I am much more interested that this money should be returned to Japan for the honor of this country and as a matter of justice than that the officers and crews should be paid. Our nation is financially not absolutely poor, but it is and must be characteristically honest. Our people seek economy, but at the same time they seek fair dealing in all our foreign as well as our private relations, and most of all do they demand that this enlightened Republic shall not take advantage of a feeble friendly power just emerging, in many respects, from the darkness of ages.

I do not believe that we shall lose anything by availing ourselves of this opportunity to perform an act of distinguished justice and magnanimity. I do not think that we can make a better mora!—and I doubt whether we can make a better material—investment. It seems to me that the political economy of those who object is summed up in the proverb of the wisest of men when he said, "There is "that scattereth and yet increaseth; and there is that withholdeth more than is "meet, but it tendeth to poverty." We shall never be poorer by performing this act of American justice.

www.ingramcontent.com/pod-product-compliance
Lightning Source LLC
Chambersburg PA
CBHW021601270326
41931CB00009B/1324